I0469149

Performance at the Highest Level

LEADERSHIP

Superior Leaders Inspire Great Performers

FOLLOWSHIP

Superb Performers Follow Passionate Leaders

STEPHEN J. BLAKESLEY

DEDICATION

For my beautiful and talented wife Lillian,
whose determination is an inspiration to me,
who labors with me, and contributes equally.

Contents

Part One: leading large

Part Two: make the next hire your best hire

Part Three: The Magnificent Seven

PART ONE

LEADING LARGE

~Six Big Ideas to Lead Exceptionally~

Stephen J. Blakesley

PROLOGUE

The purpose of Part One of this book is to share a system of *Six Big Ideas* leading to leadership excellence, a system that will set you apart from others who are aspiring to lead. One of the most important business books in the recent past is *First Break All The Rules*. This book is a "must read" for managers and leaders in both large and small organizations. There is one defining statement I will always remember, and it is essential advice for leaders everywhere—*"don't waste time trying to put into someone something that isn't there, because it is hard enough to get out what is already in."*

I, too, believe that it is more efficient and effective to focus on strengths rather than weaknesses. This book will expound on six essential steps to exceptional leadership—the *Leading Large* Six Steps System. We begin with *Big Idea One—Know Thyself.* Know the big picture and how your strengths contribute to it.

An exceptional leader will know the value of recognizing the strengths of each member of his team—will have x-ray eyes, so to speak. We'll look at this leadership role in *Big Idea Two—Have the Right Perspective. Big Idea Three—Know What's Under the Hood,* affirms that exceptional leaders know their people in a much deeper way than their average peers.

**The glue that holds Big Ideas 1, 2, and 3 together
is the leader's ability to build trust**

Big Idea Four—Build Their Trust; *Big Idea Five—Exceptional Leaders are Goal-Getters*; and finally, *Big Idea Six—Develop Emotional Intelligence Skills* to touch, inspire and lead others.

Following is the **"*Leading Large*" Six Step System to Exceptional Leadership**.

1. KNOW THYSELF
2. HAVE THE RIGHT PERSPECTIVE
3. SEE WHAT IS UNDER THE HOOD
4. BUILD TRUST
5. GOAL GETTING
6. BE EMOTIONALLY COMPETENT

The coming chapters lay out, in detail, the actions necessary for *"Leading Large."* I hope you enjoy reading "Leading Large" as much as I have enjoyed writing it.

Chapter One

BIG IDEA ONE: *Know Thyself!*

"Without a clear picture of self, it is nearly impossible to inspire others."

Leadership is a popular topic. There are over 1400 different leadership systems, and all of them involve *people*. Leadership is not so much about the leader as it is about the people who the leader must inspire to follow. *Getting people to follow you is what leadership is all about.* Creating followers begins with knowing thyself. Without a clear picture of *self*, it is nearly impossible to inspire others. People will sense an imposter. They will recognize a leader.

Most of us never take the time to clearly understand our *self*, and as a result, we often spend untold amounts of time wondering why people don't want to follow us. I have never known anyone who has not, at some point in time, wanted to get better. That applies to those who want to be the best they can be, those who want to be managers, managers who want to be a leader, and leaders who want to be better leaders. Unfortunately, some will grow, but most will not.

Robert Kelley, the author of *How to Be A Star at Work,* spent over five years on a research project that involved the most prestigious research organization in the world at the time—Bell Laboratories. Bell Labs was conspicuous about wanting, and hiring, none but the best. If you went to work for Bell Labs, you were set for life. If you had Bell Labs on your resume, it was an announcement that you were one bright dude or dudette. So Bell Labs captured none but the brightest and the best, but there was one thing wrong—they were not all performing at the "Star" level. In fact, only about 10 percent of those hired performed at a level beyond average. But that does not mean that a much larger number didn't want to perform better.

It is my belief that each person, when hired, would like to be a star—he or she wants to be "the best," but some just miss the mark. So why don't they become stars? Answer: *Because they don't know how.* They want to get better; they want to be better, but they simply do not know what to do. They lack leadership. That is the purpose of this book, to share a **System** that defines the Steps to Leadership Excellence (*Leading Large*). This system helps others comprehend their potential and teaches them how to reach it.

Leadership has become a means of creating a competitive advantage in the workplace today. Contrary to the belief of many, we are all leaders. Some in bigger ways than others, but everyone provides an example for others to follow and thus leads. Leaders do important work, whether in a family leadership role, a business role or in an organizational role. Possibly, the most important and essential work leaders do is to *inspire.* Inspired families and organizations are always winners. They stand out. They achieve. They win.

A fair question then, is, "How do I become better?" One way is to recognize the personal qualities that others notice, the qualities that lead to inspiring others. Also, to inspire others, I believe, must begin with knowing yourself. While that sounds simple enough, you would be surprised by how many fail to go deeply enough to truly understand themselves. Skill at self-evaluation is essential to a leader and often involves more than just YOU. To complete the picture, it almost always requires seeing yourself through others eyes, as well as your own.

Before you begin an effort to improve or to get better at anything, it is very important to know who you are—in your eyes and in the eyes of others. It is crucial to know your values, your behavior (at rest and under pressure), your talent and skill-level in those areas that drive performance—like emotional intelligence.

Since we may all tend to view ourselves through rose-colored glasses and sometimes believe we are somewhat better than we really are, it is important to consider the use of assessments which take your view of yourself and compare it to others' view of themselves. Two good tools, with high validity and reliability, that I depend heavily upon are: 1) Target Training International's-Trimetric, 2) Multiple Health System's EQ-i 2.0 - MSCEIT. These two assessment tools will give any manager or leader a clear picture of their own values, behavior, skills and talents. There are others but I focus on these three.

Part of their interpretation is intended to direct your attention to your strengths and weaknesses, but even more importantly, it provides a clear picture of your values, behavior, skills and talents, so that you can match them to the needs of your particular job.

A good example of the importance of *job fit* (matching your strengths and weakness with those demanded by the job) is to recognize that different jobs have different needs. If you are a person who is "introvertish" and committed to details and you step into a job needing a high level of interpersonal skills, it is highly likely that you will need to work at developing those skills or expect to be less than *star* quality. Job fit is essential to peak performance.

I am often asked, what exactly is a self-assessment? A self-assessment can be something as simple as a thoughtful review of yourself, making conclusions about your talents, knowledge and skills. That simple self-assessment can be relatively accurate on the macro scale, but is seldom detailed enough to give you adequate knowledge to craft a self-improvement program. The very best self-assessment tools are those professionally designed, scientifically maintained and digitally delivered.

The EQ-i 2.0, as an example, is one of the most highly validated and reliable self-assessment tools in the world; it measures your emotional intelligence (EI) level, a skill and a critical leadership tool. I would go so far as to say that you are not likely to become a high-performing leader without high levels of EI. The information delivered through digitally delivered assessments is invaluable.

Emotional intelligence is critical to leadership. As I have said, I do not believe it possible to lead anyone for very long without high levels of emotional intelligence. The latest research, from multiple sources, says emotional intelligence is responsible for seventy percent of a leader's success. It just makes good sense that if a major part of a leader's role is to inspire others to follow them to a predetermined destination, that emotions play a major role in communicating that destination in such a way as to inspire others. Two major needs for the emotionally intelligent leader are *Self-Awareness*, which we have already discussed, and *Empathy*.

The Self-Aware, Empathetic Leader is a real gem who understands self and can see things through others' eyes and feel what others feel. Put those two together and you have an extremely insightful individual, capable of leveraging their own talents, skills and knowledge, as well as understanding the values and motivators of others on their team. Armed with those abilities one begins to move ahead of the pack.

But the truly great leader, through self-awareness and empathy, can recognize emotions in themselves and others and manage the two for a *positive outcome*. They can do that, skillfully, because they have been trained to recognize emotions, emotional states, moods and triggers (those events that release emotions). They have learned how to communicate and convey, in an inspiring manner, the right emotions in their team.

The amount of information delivered to you, about you, through digital online assessment tools is growing daily. Most organizations use some kind of assessment tools in their selection process and many use that information for development purposes. Some people are concerned that their results would reflect poorly upon them. To that, I always encourage my clients to look at the results and remember—the results are generated by your answers to a standard list of questions. I encourage my clients to look at the results and ask themselves this question, *"Do I believe these results?"* In most cases, they do, and that is good. In those circumstances where they do not, I recommend they ask the follow-up question, *"How could that be true?"* From the answers to these questions, we often find surprises that aid us in helping the individual improve their performance.

Sometimes, however, the results just seem to be wrong, and in those cases we advise our client to ignore that particular result, but think about how it could possibly be true. I occasionally encounter people who do not wish others to view their results. The fear is that others will see weaknesses in the individual and use that knowledge to suppress their advancement. Being perfectly honest, I have never seen a case where the results were used to suppress an individual, but I have seen many cases where strengths were revealed and advancement made because of indicated strengths. I have never seen a case where the information has been used in a harmful way.

The first step to becoming a Great Leader is then, Self-Awareness. If you want to get better, first you must clearly understand who and where you are.

Often, to clearly understand who you are, and where you are, needs third party observations and opinions (coaching). No one is a perfect leader, but we can all get better. Few can see themselves clearly enough to make the changes necessary to lead in a LARGE way. Possibly, that is why coaching is such a rapidly growing profession. Helping people get better is inspirational in itself. We do believe that leaders are benefitted by coaching. Some are better at receiving and benefiting than others. Often, the first step in an effective coaching relationship is learning how to be coached, and that begins by accepting the fact that others see you differently than you see yourself, and that the view of others is important.

My most basic recommendation is—*investigate who you are and where you are by doing two things. First, take a couple of self-assessments that focus on skills, talent, behavior and values to find out where you are. Second, get a coach to help you find out who you are.*

Chapter Two

BIG IDEA TWO: *Have the Right Perspective*

"The Big Picture is all about the end result."

Leaders do not always know how they contribute to the "end game," but exceptional leaders always have the right perspective. Star performers in leadership roles not only have the right perspective, they see it clearly. Exceptional leaders know how their job contributes to the "grand plan," and how their knowledge, talents, skills and values contribute, as well. Their picture is both big and clear.

The Big Picture is all about the desired end result and how you and your work relate to others in pursuit of that desired end result. An aspiring leader, for instance, realizes that they are important and their work is important, but that it is only a part of a far bigger picture.

A leader plays a central role, as a specialist, in an often much larger, more complex machine that we call the organization. Gaining clarity about how you, a leader, fit into that larger and more complex machine does not come automatically. You have to work at it and get laser focused to clearly understand where you contribute. That work begins, I believe, with an investigation and understanding of the *culture* of the organization.

Webster's defines *culture* as the skills, arts, and beliefs of a given people during a specific time.

Within many organizations, someone, earlier, took the time to define what the organization stood for and believed in. Often times those beliefs and understandings are nicely framed and displayed in the lobby or boardroom of the organization. Sometimes they accurately reflect the organization, but more often, they are empty words that sound nice. The point is that you have to look beyond the surface of an organization—in this case, the lobby or boardroom—to understand their real culture. One of the more important descriptions of any organization's culture centers around their people; i.e., what does the organization think about its people, or possibly, does the organization even think about its people? The best source of correct answers to those questions comes from others who are part of the organization.

The sense of the people within an organization can be determined in several different ways. You can walk around with a notepad and pen and ask people questions and take good notes, or you can use a tool we found very efficient and helpful. That tool is Multiple Health System's, BOEI (Benchmark of Organization Emotional Intelligence). It is a tool that allows the employee to express their opinion, confidentially, on seven key aspects that contribute to the culture of an organization:

- *Does the organization hire people who love the work they do, then show them how they contribute to the big picture?*

- *Does the organization compensate people fairly?*
- *Is the organization concerned about work/life balance and workplace stress?*
- *Does the organization exert substantial effort toward building teams and putting people in the right places?*
- *Are the managers prepared to do the job they are supposed to do?*
- *Does the organization work to discover the talents of their people and put them in jobs where they can leverage those talents?*
- *Does the organization work at doing the right things and doing them most of the time?*

Understanding the culture of your organization is one means of knowing how you fit in. It is one thing to know the Big Picture but it is another, but equally important, to know how your talent, skills, and knowledge contribute to the Big Picture. How are your competencies and talents contributing to the end result?

I am sometimes asked the question, "What if I don't fit?" That is a good question that has a simple, two-part answer: If you don't fit, you can change or you can move on. So, really, this discussion is about two things: *Do you know your strengths and weaknesses?* How do they contribute to the accomplishment of the objectives of the organization? Bottom line— *Know the objective and how you contribute.*

These sound simple enough—having the big picture, knowing the organization, knowing where it is going, knowing yourself and how you contribute to the objective—but many leaders just don't get it. In fact, as a general rule, 80 percent or less of the workforce has that knowledge and sadly, only some of those are even identified as leaders.

Of course, knowing how you and your job contribute to the goal achievement of the organization requires self-inspection. Many simply do not take the time to get a clear picture or perspective of where they fit within the organization, and as a result, they are less effective than they should be.

There are four important steps to getting perspective (know how you fit in).

1. Step *number one*: Know yourself; know your strengths and weaknesses.
2. Step *number two*: Know your job; know what that job needs and what that job contributes.
3. Step *number three*: Know the organization, where it is going and what is needed to get there.
4. Step, *number four*: Know how your job contributes to the organizational goal or objective.

It almost seems too simple, doesn't it?
Yet, these are foundational steps to Leading Large.

CHAPTER THREE

BIG IDEA THREE: *Look Beneath The Hood*

"People are not always what they appear to be at first glance."

Exceptional leaders know their people in a much deeper way than their average peers.

If you walk onto the showroom floor of any Ford dealership, you might easily mistake the 2013 Ford Shelby GT 500 for the street version Ford Mustang Mach 5. They appear very much alike, but as you expect, they are not so much alike. For instance, the Ford Shelby is nearly a $60,000 automobile, while the Mustang Mach 5 can be had for something around $40,000. The difference doesn't stop there. You won't see the real difference until you "look beneath the hood." The Shelby has over 650 horses in there while the Mustang has only a little over 400. That is a substantial difference. I could go on, of course, but I believe I have made my point, which is develop the habit of looking beneath the hood if you want to be an exceptional leader.

Since there can be no such thing as a leader without the people who follow them, identifying likely followers and engaging them is yet another essential skill of an exceptional leader. Few will deny that *people* are the key to the success of any leader.

But, I am sure you are already beginning to see that it is not just people, but the *right people* that make a leader successful. Without the *right people* the battle is pretty much lost.

Recently, I was talking with a friend who manages a unit of a large national organization. He expressed the considerable frustration his organization is having over the startling turnover rate of 33.9 percent among 1- to 3-year tenured employees. "We must be missing it somewhere," he said. "We work real hard at attracting the smartest and brightest new hires and pay them top dollar," he continued. He ranted for several minutes and then finished by saying, "I don't think it is us; maybe it is the candidate or employee. Whadda you think?"

I shared with him the recent research findings by Dan Goleman, the author of *Primal Leadership*. In this important book the author proposes that being bright and smart might get you a job but keeping the job and advancing requires much more. He also said, "It is not IQ, but EQ, that contributes most to success on the job, at least in knowledge-based jobs." I admit that I have used a little "jargon" here and need to clarify the meaning of the two terms IQ and EQ.

IQ is an abbreviation for Intelligence Quotient, which is a phrase that describes your ability to comprehend problems presented verbally or mathematically through reading. One determines their IQ by testing, where a mean score is 100, and 95 percent of the population fall somewhere between 70 and 130 (two standard deviations on either side of the mean of 100). *Some have said that IQ is the best indicator of job performance where the applicant has no experience.* In other words, IQ is the "button" that opens the elevator door to the top. It won't get you to the top unless you press the "right button—the *EQ button.*

EQ represents what is called *Emotional Quotient,* or your level of emotional awareness, understanding and control. It is a means of determining ones emotional skills level through a self-assessment. Multiple Health Systems (the assessment distributor) identifies it as the EQi. The latest version of the EQi is the EQ-i 2.0 version, available through GMS Talent LP in Houston, TX. While IQ represents the button that opens the elevator door, EQ is that "right button," spoken of earlier, that takes you to the top.

Exceptional leadership demands emotional skills. You will not likely reach the top unless you have high levels of EQ, or emotional intelligence. Now that I have resolved the "jargon" issue, let's get back to the conversation I had with my friend who was frustrated because he and others in his organization were not able to reach their hiring, retention and production goals.

It is safe to begin with the statement that a leader's success is often determined by the quality and engagement of the people he selects or woos for his team. Certainly, a high level of EQ would be very important in a candidate, but there are other things that matter, too.

For instance, it is important that any leader or organization have a clear picture of what the important jobs call for regarding talents, skill, values and behavior. Equally important is the need for clarity around the expectations of the job.

As an executive search firm, we see a lot of gaps in the organization's description of job expectations. Without knowing what the real expectations of the job are, it is difficult, if not impossible, to achieve them. Exceptional leaders will clearly define the expectations of every job in their unit.

Time demands on the leader are instrumental in the encouragement of short cuts that often result in disaster. A good example of how that plays out is when an important position is vacant and a leader is pressured to fill the position quickly. In doing so he/she often ends up buying time only for a short while but at a very high price. The position may get filled and look fine for a little while until the performance of that "quick hire" has time to come to light. *Shortcuts in hiring are almost always disastrous.*

My friend admitted that often, hiring people takes a "backseat" to the latest and most urgent problem that arises, and that they spend a lot of time putting the "train back on the track." We continued to talk, and I had an opportunity to share with him the importance of having a system to find, hire, develop and keep good people. "My firm has developed two systems that help you make the right decisions without really thinking too much," I said. "The *Strategic Hiring* system and *The Target* are two systems that help with the selection, hiring and development of people. "It boils down to this," I shared. "There are just three rules that exceptional leaders follow to get spectacular results."

- *Know what you want from the job*
- *Know what it will take to get what you want*
- *Get to know your people in ways they do not expect*

To that last point above, the part about getting to know your people, I continued by telling him the story of the time I cultivated and coached an organization to walk-the-talk about getting to know their people in an unusual but powerfully successful way.

We developed a program and policy among all managers that they *must* (with emphasis) build and keep what they called "The Book" on each employee. The Book was a detailed record of each direct report, a record of important dates, family names, achievements, goals, anniversaries and hopes to be used as a reference tool each time the manager met with the employee. The purpose, of course, was to provide a resource to the manager that would allow a more personal approach to the people they led and managed. It worked.

This organization, a sales organization, soon had one of the lowest turnover ratios and highest productivity rate of any company with which I have ever worked.

Numerous times I have had their employees tell me, in direct coaching sessions, how much they loved to work for this organization and how thankful they were to work with their manager. I cannot be totally sure, of course, but the reason I believe this approach worked so well was due to the way each manager/wannabe leader was instructed to gather the information. Thanks to the leadership of the Founder and the President (two different people) we were able to create for this organization a very structured management-training program with instructions on how to "build The Book." The key to accurate and meaningful information for The Book was a personal interview with each manger, giving them training on how to conduct the interview that was to be held away from the office, without alcohol and in a comfortable and safe place. The manager/leader wannabe was instructed to build a relationship with each employee by sending the message that they really cared about them, as a person, thus the need for personal information.

Exceptional leadership requires a "High Touch."

CHAPTER FOUR

BIG IDEA FOUR: *Build Their Trust!*

"Survey of Trust in the Workplace" (2010), revealed that almost half (48%) of those surveyed, planned to leave their organization because of declining trust."

Americans cast a vote of trust every few years. We elect a President, a Senator or a Representative to go to Washington D. C. and represent us in important matters that affect all our lives. We express our trust by casting a ballot. We elect people (place our trust in people) to represent us in matters of government. We trust the people we elect to express our beliefs and work toward our goals.

The last time I checked, only about 13 percent of us believed that our elected federal official—the person we trusted—deserved that trust. Put another way, that is less than two people out of ten in this country believe they elected the right person to represent them in very important matters.

In corporate matters, at work, where most of us spend more of our time than any place else, no polls have been taken, or shared, about whether job leaders do what they are supposed to do. In fact, we don't even get to pick our leaders at work. We are often assigned leaders that represent others' point of view,

Stephen J. Blakesley

not ours. Some recent research presented by Stephen M.R. Covey and his organization, showed that only 49% of employees trust senior management and only 28% believe CEOs are a credible source of information. If a similar survey were taken within the financial markets, today, the trust would likely be even lower.

According to the Deloitte LLP "Survey of Trust in the Workplace" (2010), nearly half (48%) of those surveyed planned to leave their organization because of declining trust. Another surprising finding was that only 65% of executives believe that trust impacts performance within their organization. I could go on and on about the value of trust and its apparent decline, but let's get positive.

Few would argue with me about the value and importance of trust. It is especially important among leaders. Kouzes and Posner, in their book, *Leadership Excellence*, express "integrity" (trusting people to do what they say they will do) as one of the five all-time most admired traits of leaders around the world. Is it any wonder, then, that the subject of trust and how to build it would be important to leadership excellence? There are, of course, many ways in which one might build trust. Here's a list of important Trust Builders:

First on the list is a commitment to *Integrity*. Integrity in a corporate leader is simply *doing what you say you will do*. Saying, "I am going to get you that raise," for instance, and then getting it is a good example of integrity. Or, "No more working on weekends," and sticking to it is another. "We will have that report on your desk by Friday," then having it there on Thursday is yet another good example of integrity. *Trust is built on a foundation of Integrity.*

Second on my list of trust-builders is **Listening**. There are no college courses on listening. You have to learn it on your own. All too frequently, a leader's ability to talk overwhelms their need to listen. I think the idea, "none of us are as smart as all of us," is a good thought here. You can't hear what others have knowledge of while you are talking. Not always, but frequently, the best ideas for solving a problem come from others, and we can't hear those ideas if we are talking. Listening also sends an important message: "I care about what you think and say." Knowing that someone really cares about your thoughts and ideas is a big trust builder.

Third on the list of important trust-builders is ***Accountability***. Accountability is different from Integrity in that Integrity is about doing what you say you will do and Accountability is about raising the "Stop! The buck-stops-here" sign. Taking the blame is the responsibility of the leader. A willingness to step up and accept the responsibility for a failed effort or program is rare among leaders and distances those who do it from those who don't.

Fourth on the list of trust-builders is showing ***Respect*** for others. All too often leaders forget that they would not be leaders were it not for followers. Sometimes leaders forget that there would be no leaders without followers and that the followers do most of the real work in any organization. Showing respect for the individual and team is an essential action necessary for building trust.

Fifth on the list of trust-building leadership essentials is *Loyalty*. Loyalty cannot really come without physical involvement. To demonstrate loyalty a leader must be actively involved in the achievement of the objective. They must be willing to take the blame if the project fails, give praise when warranted and they must be willing to stand behind the decisions of their team, even if the decisions are wrong.

Trust in business has been on the decline for several years. According to Fast Company, trust in our corporate leaders took a nosedive in 2009 and reached its lowest level in 2012. Some organizations and their leaders, however, have maintained a higher level of trust, not by accident, but because they recognized the value of trust building and worked at it. Those organizations, according to the "Trust in Business" survey, enjoy an unusually strong P/E ratio, often as much as 25% higher than their not-so-trustworthy competitors.

So, devoting time to understanding the importance of trust and how to get it is of significant value to the organization, the leader and the follower. A quick review of the *Five Ways Exceptional Leaders Build Trust* will be time well spent.

Five Sure-fire Ways You, as a Leader, Can Build Trust among your team:

- Build Your Integrity
- Learn World-class Listening
- Be Accountable
- Show Respect for Others
- Be Loyal

Building Your Integrity
Integrity is all about doing what you say you will do. The first step in making that easier is to think before you commit. Do not commit to do more than you are capable of doing. The second step is to plan ahead—set milestones that lead to you keeping your commitment. And third is about staying focused—help your team stay focused on the target, the goal and the due date.

Learn World-class Listening
You are not likely to find any organized advanced learning classes on *listening,* so you must be practical. Be serious about learning to be a good listener. To be a good listener, you must first assume that others have a desire to be of value and make a relevant contribution. When others are speaking, you turn to them, make eye contact, display positive body language, take notes, if possible, and finally, thank them.

Be Accountable
Remember! YOU are the leader and YOU are responsible for the outcome. As Harry Truman said, "The buck stops here." Leaders must prepare themselves to receive negative feedback when projects fail or falter and be prepared to tacitly enjoy victories, giving the credit to the team, when things go right.

Show Respect for Others
Leaders should remind themselves that few, if any, of their visions or dreams would ever be achieved were it not for others (the followers). In fact, they would not even be leaders were it not for others who choose to follow. Know how members of

your team contribute to the organization, and thank them for it on a regular basis.

Be Loyal

Be someone your team can count on. Help keep them from trouble. Lift them up when others are pushing them down. Be transparent and avoid hidden agendas. Remember the "grapevine" grows but does not always put out world-class grapes. Be known for your caring conduct. Your achievements will speak for themselves.

Your ability to build trust among potential followers opens the door to exceptional leadership.

CHAPTER FIVE

BIG IDEA FIVE: *Make It Goal Getting*

*"Entrepreneurs, business owners and managers:
goal getting is the "starting gun."*

Exceptional leaders are not relied upon to set goals; they are called upon to **make** goals. **Exceptional leaders** are Goal-Getters.

Setting a goal is powerful, but *getting* a goal is even more so. Of course, setting a goal is an essential part of getting a goal, but not nearly as much fun, right? For entrepreneurs, business owners and managers, goal getting is the "starting gun." Sharing what I have learned about goal getting over the years is my purpose, so here is a true story to get us started.

When I was seven (that would be 2nd grade), my Uncle Orville (I called him Uncle Orv) was a high school coach in Cordell, Oklahoma, and I admired him so much. That year, he and his football team came to Watonga (my hometown) to play the Eagles in football. Cordell was not in our District, so the Eagles did not play them often. I don't remember the outcome of the game, but I do remember clearly the time he spent with me that evening at our house, after the game.

You see, high school football games were mostly played on Friday evenings and often Saturday was reserved for the kid's game. We played on the grade school yard every Saturday morning after the Eagles played a home game. It was our time to play like we were the Eagles, and I asked my Uncle Orv, who being a football coach had all the answers, to give me some special plays so my team could win on Saturday. He gave me two of the most fantastic plays you could ever imagine, and we did win the sandlot game that Saturday. But the thing I remember most about that evening with Uncle Orv was what he said to me.

He said—and I remember so clearly—"One day soon, you will play for real, possibly for the University of Oklahoma." I cannot tell you how many times I thought about and dreamed about that statement, because anybody who wanted to play college football knew of the University of Oklahoma and their coach Bud Wilkenson. That comment was the seed of a goal that taught me what, I believe, is one of the most important lessons in life—***Goals are the fuel that moves us to achieve.*** Without a clear and powerful goal it is difficult to know the direction in which we should go. I will tell you how this goal played out later, but for now I want to share with you a thought by a mentor of mine:

> ***"We all need lots of powerful long-range goals to help us past the short-term obstacles."***
> **– Jim Rohn**

Certainly, we all encounter obstacles in our journey through life. It is just sad to know that some allow short-term obstacles to become long-term roadblocks simply because they never learn the value of, and method of, setting clear, powerful, long-term goals. So, let's talk about the process of setting goals first, and then the "getting" of those goals. Brian Tracey, one of the most prolific writers on goals and their value in the entire world said, "Your ability to set goals is the master skill of success." What got my attention was the word "master." To me that means, "Pay attention and do this." If you want to be an exceptional leader, you must have clear goals.

As a big goal-setter, over the years I have developed a system, while not perfect, it has been very effective. The system is not just about goal setting but about goal getting, which is the purpose of setting goals.

There are three things you must have to be successful at getting goals. None of us wants to set targets or goals that we never act upon or achieve. We want to **set** a goal and **get** it!

The **first** of the three things needed for goal getting is a *clear, well-defined goal*. Fuzzy, general goals just will not work here or anywhere for that matter. So, spend time getting clarity around your goal.

The **second** is an *irrational exuberance* for achieving the goal. If you do not have passion for achieving your goal, the likelihood of achieving it is remote.

The **third** need for effective goal getting is to *know the price you will have to pay to get it and decide if you are willing to pay it. If you are not willing to pay the price, don't even begin. The results will be disastrous and you will have wasted a lot of time and effort.

Stephen J. Blakesley

How should we refine our goals so that they are crystal clear? Getting crystal clear goals begins with identifying what you really want. Two things I hear frequently when I ask people what they want are *Happiness* and *Success*. Both are worthy objectives but not distilled enough to be called clear goals. Both of these need further clarification. Crystal clear goals are ones that engage our subconscious honing device and keep us moving toward them—even when we are not actively thinking about them. They must be clear and concise.

For instance, if happiness is an important goal of yours, you should be able to answer the question, "What makes me happy?" What makes you happy must be clear and singular. It is difficult for the subconscious mind to focus on more than one thing at a time. The ability to achieve a goal diminishes proportionally with the number of goals on which the subconscious is asked to focus. My recommendation is get a yellow pad and pen and ask yourself, or have someone ask you, "What do you want?" Write down the answer. Keep asking yourself the same question until you cannot think of anything else you want. Then from that list, pick one thing that you want the most. That is getting clear about what you want.

Maybe it is $10,000. Maybe the $10,000 is to pay your electric bill or pay off your mortgage. It doesn't really matter as long as that is what you want more than anything else on your list. You now have a clear goal, but there is one more thing that needs to happen before this becomes a clear and powerful goal—attach a date. When do you want this $10,000? I suspect that most of us could use the $10,000 anytime we could get it, but if you do not have it, give yourself a reasonable amount of time to get it.

38

Whatever that is, write it down next to the $10,000. You have just thrown the switch to your God-given subconscious device. Maxwell Maltz, the author of *Psycho-Cybernetics,* calls it your Automatic Success Mechanism. It works 24/7 to take you where you most want to go. Congratulations on creating such a clear goal-getter and throwing the switch on your ASM (Automatic Success Mechanism).

The fuel for this special God-given tool (your ASM) is "passion" (irrational exuberance). So let's "call up" the passion (develop the irrational exuberance) for this very specific, clear goal you just set, by asking the following question: Why do I want this? What will I do with it when I get it, and how will it benefit me or how will I enjoy it when I get it? Picture yourself, in the minutest detail, doing the things that achieving the goal would allow you to do. Now that we have the clarity and the passion, we're good to go.

The final step in goal getting is to know what you are willing to pay to get what you want. Knowing the price you are willing to pay is often the determining factor in getting the goal. A good example is, you want an Olympic gold medal in gymnastics and you are really passionate about getting that Olympic gold medal. You investigate and find that it takes a minimum of 10 years of practice and training, every day, and that is just what gets you to a place where you might be selected to try out for the Olympic team. Still no guarantee you will get the medal, just the opportunity to try to get the medal. You begin looking at your life and the things you want to do and see that you are not willing to commit so much time and effort simply for an opportunity to get your goal. That is what I mean by checking to see if you are willing to pay the price. Admittedly, we cannot always determine the price, and sometimes we press ahead toward a goal only to spend time and effort and then realize we are not willing to commit any more. The result is many years and much effort wasted that could have been spent doing something else you are passionate about that does not have such a high price. The bottom line here is to look at the goal, double check your passion for it, and ask yourself if you are willing to pay the price you perceive necessary to pay to get your goal.

Two things to close this conversation about goals: First, Mark McCormack, in his book, *What They Don't Teach You at Harvard Business School,* tells of a survey of MBA graduates, which asked, "Do you have clear, written goals for your future and have you made plans to accomplish them?" Only 3 % had written goals and plans to achieve them; thirteen percent had goals, but not in writing, and 84 percent had no goal at all. Ten years later, the same people were interviewed and it was found that the 13 percent who had goals, but not in writing, were earning twice as much as the 84 percent who had no goal at all. Most astonishingly, the 3 percent that had written goals were earning ten times more than the other 97 percent of the graduates.

Second, I promised to finish my personal story at the beginning of the chapter. The story was about a goal I set for myself at the early age of seven to play college football. My goal was to play college football at the University of Oklahoma. Well, I did not make that goal, but I did win a scholarship to play college football at Oklahoma State University, and I played on the only

OSU freshman team to beat the University of Oklahoma freshman, ever. I did not get everything I wanted, but I did get much of it. I would never have achieved that much without being passionate about a real, clear goal.

Stephen J. Blakesley

CHAPTER SIX

BIG IDEA SIX: *Be Emotionally Competent*

**"Emotional competence is understanding your emotions
and the application or management of them."**

Exceptional Leaders are emotionally aware of themselves and others—they are capable of managing their emotions. As pointed out in previous writings, "Emotional intelligence (EI) accounts for 85 – 90 percent of the difference between average leaders and their more average peers," a quote from the book *Resonant Leadership* by Richard Boyatzis and Anne McKee. If you look up the definition of the word "intelligence," you will find intelligence means understanding. So, the term "emotional intelligence" means emotional understanding, not just yourself, but also understanding those who work with you. The term "emotional competence" implies not only understanding of emotions but the application or management of emotions, as well.

I do know, for certain, that no individual can be an exceptional leader without being emotionally competent. How do we become emotionally competent? If you want to be an exceptional leader, you cannot do it without being emotionally competent. As stated earlier, emotional competence requires not only the understanding of emotions but the management of emotions within yourself and others. The path to emotional understanding and management begins with ourselves and then moves to others.

Most of us are aware of just a few emotions that we experience frequently, like *fear, sadness* or *happiness*. But emotions are much more complex than just those few frequently experienced feelings. There are eight core emotions and there are derivations and combinations that form far more than just those eight emotional states. Possibly as many as 30 or even more are experienced over a short period of time.

As a leader, it is important not only to know emotions but to understand the source of them. For instance, emotions are hardwired in humans—hardwired meaning that they come naturally and most frequently without effort on our part. Emotions are chemical reactions that occur in the brain, instigating physiological reactions in the body that enhance our ability to protect the body. A good example might be the emotion of *fear* that could be brought on by the site of a rattlesnake near a small child. Blood flows to the stomach and is redirected to other parts of the body to provide fuel for muscle parts that would allow you to grab a hoe and chop the snake in a million pieces or run quickly to snatch the child away from the encounter. The main thing to remember is that emotions are chemical reactions that cause physiological changes in the body to produce a certain protective behavior.

Left uncontrolled, emotions can cause havoc. Learning to control your emotions can be a powerful tool and one that makes great leaders. Also, understanding that emotion impacts the way we see ourselves and others, how we manage stress, how we make decisions, and how effectively we communicate with others—this is knowledge that has great leverage. For instance, being able to recognize emotion in others simply by observing facial expression and understanding that emotion enhances or diminishes our communication with others is a valuable skill, whether you are a leader or not. Recognizing that many emotions are triggered by certain sounds, sights or smells and that emotions impact the way people behave is invaluable knowledge for a leader. So the basic steps a leader might take to raise their level of emotional skills begins with knowledge about emotion, and then knowledge about how emotion affects certain beliefs and behavior among ourselves and others. This has great value.

To begin, a leader or wannabe leader needs a clear understanding of how they react to emotion. One of the most used tools for that purpose is a self-assessment known as the EQi 2.0, distributed by Multiple Health Systems and administered by professionals around the world. This tool is useful in determining strengths and weaknesses. It is beneficial to see how others perceive you in the emotional area and compare their perception with yours. The EQ 360 is a valuable tool for that, also. Another tool is to measure your knowledge about the impact of emotion on performance and is useful to spot the weaknesses in your understanding. That tool is called the MISCEIT and is distributed, again, by MHS in Toronto, Canada. There are a few other EI measurement tools but our time and space is limited here.

I find that leaders sometimes have difficulty knowing how to use emotional intelligence to improve business results. For that purpose, I recommend the book, *The Emotionally Intelligent Manager*, by David Caruso and Peter Salovey. They lay out a very practical four-step process of using emotional knowledge to raise personal performance and corporate profits. The four steps are: Identify Emotions, Use Emotions, Understand Emotions, and Manage Emotions. These four steps provide a means for you to develop your emotional skills, and most importantly, teach you how to engage emotions to improve business results. Let's look at each one separately.

Identify Emotions

Learning to recognize and identify emotions can often be best accomplished by learning the "triggers" that bring emotions on. Maybe just keeping a yellow pad on your desk for a couple of weeks and drawing a line down the middle and every time you experience an emotion, try to identify it among the core emotions of Anger, Sadness, Happiness, Fear, Disgust, Surprise, Trust and Anticipation. And then simultaneously, attempt to identify a trigger. A trigger is the event that caused the emotion. In a very short period of time you will identify those emotions that you most frequently deal with and learn what caused them.

Using Emotions

There are very strong links between emotions and our thought process. I am sure we have all experienced times when our emotional state has helped or hindered our thinking and behavior. Positive and negative thinking rouses emotional states that impact our thought and decision-making process. For instance *happiness or joy* is a core emotion. Think of the different views we often get when we are in a happy mood versus a sad mood. Often, we find we are more creative, can and do think outside the box and are simply able to generate more ideas when we are happy. Happiness is a particularly important emotion to leaders. Since leaders can only be such (leaders that is) if they have followers, try to remember when you have seen people racing to be around negative or pessimistic people. Not very often, I'll bet. Learning to use emotions is not hard, but it does require thought and consideration.

Understanding Emotions
What exactly does that mean? That is a very good question. Let me put it like this: It is all about understanding what emotions are and what they cause. "Emotions warn us of possible danger or of good things to come," say Caruso and Salovey. Most of us are left to learn how to deal with emotions on our own. Some of us learn and some don't.

Let's just focus on a few core emotions, what they mean, and what is likely to follow those emotions. Exceptional leaders understand emotions and their power. *Anger*, for instance, arises out of a sense of injustice or wrong. Without anger we might tolerate prejudice or injustice. That's the good side of anger. The bad side is anger can lead to violence. Leaders can raise anger in others by emotional speech, causing mob mentality. So you might say that there is a good and bad side of anger.

Happiness moves us to embrace and receive others. Happiness is a signal to pay attention to what is going on around us. We are happy when we win a race or achieve a goal. Happiness inspires us to more. Happiness motivates.

Fear sends signals that something bad is about to happen. Often, we fear things that never happen. Fear affects our behavior whether it happens or not. Fear and anxiety bring on stress and stress kills.

Surprise occurs when things unexpected happen and when things expected don't happen. Surprise brings our attention into focus. Surprise causes us to pay attention.

Sadness is often brought about by a loss of some kind—a loss of someone or something. Sadness occurs when we fail to reach a goal and often brings about a mourning period where people feel justified in doing nothing but being remorseful. When we are sad, we are often so internally focused that we are no threat to others. It often signals others that we need help or support of some kind.

So, understanding emotions and what they cause provides leaders with insight they would not otherwise have had.

Managing Emotions

Possibly the most important thing we need to know about emotions is that they often signal to us the existence of a real issue or problem. Remember that emotions are what God gave us to help direct our thinking to what is important. The key to managing emotions is being sensitive to their presence and knowing the message they send. Here are some thoughts about how you might become more sensitive to emotions:

- *Among the core emotions, identify the ones that give you the most trouble.*
- *Make a list of emotional triggers.*
- *Learn to generate calm and pleasant moods.*

Another opportunity to manage emotions comes with the recognition that *moods* follow emotions, and while they are milder, they last much longer. Recognize that moods have an impact on our emotions. For instance, if we are in a bad or negative mood, we will react to anger quicker.

Learning how to manage anger, for instance, will have a major impact on our image to others. We haven't even touched on the power of managing emotions in others. A great example of managing emotion in others lies in motivation. Providing an atmosphere where people feel encouraged to be the best they can be is a powerful tool. Exceptional leaders are masters at managing emotions in others.

Being emotionally competent is dually dependent upon understanding and managing emotions. It is a skill and can be learned. So, the "ball is in your court." You can choose *to be, or not to be—emotionally intelligent.*

> *"Whether you believe you can or can't, you're right."*
> *-Henry Ford*

In this section of the book, I have shared with you Six Big Ideas that create Exceptional Leaders. I have given you many tips that allow you to use your motions—as a leader and to be exceptional. What you do with the information is up to you.

References—Part One

Prologue
Marcus Buckingham and Curt Coffman, *First Break All the Rules,* Simon and Schuster, NY, NY.

Big Idea #One
Robert Kelley, *How to Be a Star at Work,* Times Books, NY, NY.

Big Idea #Two
Dr. Steven Stein, *The EQ Edge*, Jossey Bass, San Francisco, CA

Big Idea #Three
Dan Goleman, Richard Boyatzis, and Anne McKee, *Primal Leadership,* Harvard Business School Press, Boston, Mass.

Big Idea #Five
Richard Boyatzis and Anne McKee, *Resonant Leadership,* Harvard Business School Press, Boston, Mass.

Big Idea #Six
David Caruso and Peter Salovey, *The Emotionally Intelligent Manager*, Jossey Bass, San Francisco, CA.

PART TWO

MAKE THE NEXT HIRE
YOUR BEST HIRE

~Hire the right person the first time using the
Strategic Hiring System©~

ACKNOWLEDGEMENTS

I want to thank authors Curt Coffman and Marcus Buckingham, who wrote the great business book, *"First Break All The Rules,"* and Leigh Branham, who wrote *"Keeping the People Who Keep You In Business."* I would also like to thank Target Training International for the great research that was referenced in this Part Two section of the book.

INTRODUCTION

By the time you finish reading Part Two of this book, you will know how to hire better people and how to make certain they fit the job. In doing so, you guarantee yourself and your organization higher productivity and higher profits!

History is full of stories about extraordinary achievements. Many are accounts of remarkable performances by groups of people, banded together for a common purpose. Their purpose might have been to win a game, fight a war, or build a business. Regardless of the purpose, the fundamentals of building a superior performing team remain essentially the same.

Warren Bennis and Patricia Ward Biederman refer to these teams as "Great Groups" in their book, *Organizing Genius*. They point to the impact that carefully selected people, led by unique individuals, have on the results of an organization. In an earlier book, *Strategic Hiring—Tomorrow's Benefits Today,* I wrote, "*Many organizations want, but do not have, high-performing people.*" It is not just about "*wanting to have;*" it's more about "*doing to have.*"

Want to build a "Great Group?" **Read on!**

53

Unfortunately, putting together a "Great Group" is not as simple as it may seem. When I was only eight and charged with the responsibility of putting together the "Saturday Morning" football team (another Great Group), it was simply a matter of choosing from my peers the fastest or the biggest or the meanest. As the opposing team's captain and I stood facing the possible candidates, we both knew that the outcome of the game would be determined by a flip of a coin, not by any secret play or great strategy. We both knew that whoever got the first pick, would pick Fred and the team with Fred would win.

Fred had been "held back" not one, but two years. Not only had Fred been held back, he had experienced an unusual spurt of growth and was close to 6 feet tall at just 11 years of age. Further, Fred's unusual size did not diminish his speed. He ran like the wind, and every offensive play consisted of the quarterback taking the ball on three and pitching to Fred on a "right sweep" or a "left sweep," which resulted in touchdown after touchdown. Let me also say that you did not try to tackle Fred, because if he got up to even "half speed," it took many more than one of us to bring Fred down. It was just too much punishment.

So, who won or lost Saturday's game really boiled down to a coin toss. We would decide who got first pick by flipping a coin. And whoever got first pick got Fred, and whoever got Fred was going to win. The point is, according to the Wall Street Journal, organizations are no more successful in finding the right people and getting them in the right jobs using their current selection methods than they would be if they simply tossed a coin.

A 50% success rate is an alarming number and it becomes even more alarming when you consider that the cost of replacing even a minimum wage employee is $10,000. The cost of replacing a manager can be as high as $100,000, and the replacement of a key executive can exceed $250,000. With those kinds of dollars involved, some attention directed to selection and retention is urgently warranted, wouldn't you say?

Yet, with hiring failures and increasing turnover on the rise, fewer than ten percent of our corporate organizations have priority plans to improve the hiring and retention process. Reducing turnover rests in two primary processes: Hiring a person with talent and seeing that the person gets in a job position that fits their talent. Achieving these two objectives will, without question, **reduce turnover** and **improve profits**.

My purpose, then, is to share with you a system for hiring talented people that has been tested in the "crucible" of real business competition. Through thirty years of searching for top candidates and hiring them, I have found many things that work, but few that work all the time. For those who want to put together a "Great Group," it does take more than the toss of a coin, but you can still have "Fred" on your team. The *Strategic Hiring System* and Fred are much alike. Both will guarantee a win if they are part of your game plan.

It is true that remarkable outcomes begin with incredible people. Yet, few businesses ever take the time to develop a system that insists on superior people. Rushing past this critical step in company building has cost millions of dollars, "burned" many a great hire and generally slowed the company's growth process to a snail's pace.

Further, many entrepreneurial types burn precious capital that could be used for growth by "flat out" hiring the wrong people. It is my contention that most hiring mistakes are a result of poor planning and organization. It is the old "**ready, fire, aim**" approach. The *Strategic Hiring System©* presented for you here is the solution to many organization needs. Here are a few ways you will benefit from reading this section of the book:

- **You will no longer be frustrated by hiring choices**
- **You will be able to listen to the job speak**
- **Your will know for certain the needs to fill any job**
- **You will save hundreds of thousands of dollars**
- **You will increase productivity as much as seven times**
- **You will be a champion to your best people**

I could go on, but why don't you find out for yourself. Get the tools *that will make a difference in your organization.* Put the SHS on your team!

PROLOGUE

Hiring successfully is no easy task. It is part science and part intuition. In the pages that follow, you will capture the knowledge that you want and need to become a better business owner, manager or executive. You will learn that it is possible to *hire the right person the first time.*

The *Strategic Hiring System©* (**SHS**) is *zero theory* and *all practical application of known facts*. The **SHS** is a hiring and selection system that works in small and large organizations alike. The **SHS** takes all the guesswork out of hiring. No more "mini-me" hiring decisions. No more dreading the interviewing process, and most of all, no more fear of making the wrong decision on the "all important hire." In all, the **SHS** is every hiring manager's dream. The **SHS** enhances success and reduces fear of making the wrong decision. The *"Strategic Hiring System"* from GMS Talent L P is your key to enhanced productivity and increased profits!

CHAPTER ONE

THE BEGINNING

It was 1981, in Houston, Texas. Just a few short years before, Houston had been a boomtown. I remember many discussions about whether or not the boom in Houston would ever end. The consensus was that it would not. We were wrong.

In only a very few months, the price of oil had dropped from forty dollars a barrel to only ten. The ripples of that event quickly impacted almost every sector of the local economy. Possibly the greatest impact was felt in the banking and real estate industries. The reality of what was happening prompted commercial developers to build hundreds of shopping centers for ghost tenants. However, none of the ghost tenants showed up to pay the rent. Thousands of square feet of retail space lay vacant for months and years.

A similar story was unfolding among the multi-story office buildings in the city. They were beautiful; they were pleasing to the eye; they were supported by big mortgages—but they were empty. There had never been a better time to rent office space in Houston. The only problem—there was *no one who wanted to rent office space.*

Eventually, of course, the house of cards, (the banks and builder/developers who had been doing the building) began to crumble. The shopping centers and high-rise office buildings could not be sold to a speculative buyer. The mortgage money had dried up, and the Savings and Loan debacle was just around the corner. These were the times that birthed one of the most effective hiring systems in the history of the insurance industry. This hiring system is so effective and universally applicable that I want to share it with you.

Most business-owners, Human Resources managers, and entrepreneurs hire to fill a position. When a job is open they move quickly to fill it. Often, little or no forethought is given to the requirements of the job, the outcomes expected, or what a person's abilities are in terms of knowledge, skills or talents that are necessary to fill a vacancy—much less, be a superior performer in it. Almost certainly, little or no thought is given to the organization's "Core Values" and the "Ideal Candidate Profile." As a result, *turnover* becomes a major expense factor. Yet, it never shows on the Profit and Loss sheet because there is never a *turnover line item*.

Researchers believe that the tangible and intangible costs of replacing people can range from as little as $10,000 for the replacement of an hourly employee, to as much as three times the annual salary for a key employee or sales person. My experience has been that most executives or business owners are either not aware of the magnitude of the problem or just don't care. They are not aware, because the impact of the problem on the bottom line is hard to trace.

Regardless of whether you are running an organization of two or two thousand, building a High Performing Team demands your attention. If someone were to ask you to explain your hiring system, what would you say? Most businesses don't have a system other than *if the job is vacant, fill it as fast as you can.* The smaller the business, the less likely they will have a formal hiring process. Yet, the single most important activity of any business is the hiring of quality people. The failure to have a process for hiring is tantamount to *willing failure.*

We used to wander aimlessly through the hiring process. It is true that necessity is the mother of invention. One day in 1983, one of our key insurance carriers, through whom we placed over 60 percent of our business, came to us with an ultimatum: "Get Profitable or we are pulling our commitment to your agency."

At that time the turnover ratio of our agency force was 38 percent annually. I had known for years that something needed to be done about it, but I kept putting it off. At the encouragement of our key carrier, I could not afford to put it off any longer. To address the problem I developed a plan of attack and called it the *"Strategic Hiring System."* That plan was so successful—I want to share it with you.

The *"Strategic Hiring System"* (SHS) was developed to reduce turnover and do it fast (**we reduced turnover from 38 percent annually to 8 percent annually in one year. The Estimated value annually was $300,000**). The resulting benefits of the SHS (in addition to the $300,000 just mentioned) were many, but here are just a few:

Stephen J. Blakesley

The Strategic Hiring Systems benefits:

- Provides a clear and easy path to follow to improve the quality of hire.
- Simplifies the process of matching candidate skills with the need of the job—and that's any job.
- Enables you to create a richness into your hiring process that sets your organization apart from your competition.
- Allows you to easily compare candidates, their talents, skills and knowledge.
- Improves the performance and retention of the hire due to better job-fit.
- Provides an accountability tool for the *first 90 days and beyond.*
- Includes interview questions with answers and scoring.

These are just a few benefits; there are many more.

The SHS is divided into NINE distinctive parts for easy organization and application.

Step I: Develop a Performance-Based Job Description

Step II: Develop the Ideal Candidate Profile

Step III: Develop a Job Benchmark

Step IV: The Telephone Interview

Step V: Assess The Candidate's Emotional Intelligence

Step VI: Plan the Opening Interview

Step VII: Assess the Candidate's Skills Capacity, Values, And Behavior

Step VIII: Conduct the Selection Interview

Step IX: Determine Job-Fit and Make an Offer

The **SHS** is not limited to any particular size of the organization and can be used universally in any hiring effort. Before we get into the system itself, there are a *few other tools* we need to get out and sharpen.

First, prepare a brief "elevator speech" that describes your company and why anyone would want to work there. Keep it brief and to the point. I suggest memorizing it so that the same thing is said to each candidate.

Second, prepare core questions for each interview and the answers to look for.

Third, make decisions about who will conduct the interview and who will observe. Ideally, there should be an interviewer and an observer.

The elevator speech is an important tool, and many large companies have presentations using fine quality videos or other multimedia presentations. Smaller companies and entrepreneurial efforts should also have something prepared to give to prospective employees. They need the personal touch of verbal communication. As an example, time should be devoted to the development of two, three-to-five-minute commentaries on the culture of the company, a description of the position or opportunity, and a discussion of why others want to work for the company. Of course, the interviewer should internalize these brief talks for use in the initial interview.

This single effort will make a tremendous difference in your hiring results. You don't need to worry about forgetting part of the presentation because the candidate doesn't have the script and will never know if you left out the paragraph about the lunchroom. The advantage is that you will not have to worry about what you are going to say and can focus on listening to the candidate's answers.

Advance preparation of the interview questions is another critical task. It is, possibly, the single most important duty of the interviewer. **Be prepared to listen** and take notes. Listening has been said to be the opposite of "preparing to talk." Few people can listen to the response of a candidate if they are thinking of what they will ask next. It just makes good sense for the interviewer to have questions prepared before the interview begins. In doing so, they can then fully listen to the responses of the candidate.

The interviewer should prepare the questions. In other words, there are specific questions for the *"Telephone Interview,"* the *"Opening Interview,"* and the *"Selection Interview."* The questions should be prepared so that the interviewer can make notes regarding the candidate's answers along with the interviewer's observations.

Some companies like to have different interviewers interview the same candidate. There is great value in multiple perspectives. However, it is my preference to get that perspective through observation as opposed to participation. My approach has always been to involve an observer but maintain continuity with regard to who leads the interview. The interview should always involve the potential manager of the candidate and another hiring manager observer. My recommendation is that the hiring manager act as an observer in the "Selection Interview." The observer technique brings a different perspective to the table and brings personalities together that may be working together on common projects in the future.

At this point we are ready to begin drilling deeper into the *"Strategic Hiring System."* Every hire is different and for that reason, two special tools, if developed properly, will allow you to apply the **SHS** to every hire, at every level. The "Ideal Candidate Profile" and the "Performance Based Job Description" are both essential tools that enhance the system and promote its flexibility.

Chapter Two

THE PERFORMANCE BASED JOB DESCRIPTION

One thing positive that came out of the 80s in Houston was an overwhelming supply of competent people looking for work. The place was crawling with college grads from the banking, petroleum, and real estate markets. They all had great work history and most were fed-up with corporate America. They were looking for a career change and many were looking for entrepreneurial opportunities.

We were aggressively growing our market-share, and these people looked like the entrepreneurial types we were looking for. They seemed to be the right people to grow remote insurance offices and become independent business-owners. Boy! Were we in for a surprise. Recruiting and hiring these people was easy. Seeing them achieve success was another thing. Our retention of selected candidates was only about 60 percent.

Not only were they failing almost as fast as they were being hired, they were poisoning the sea of future candidates. They would come on board and within six months to a year, they were not only through, but they were telling all their buddies how difficult it was to succeed. That, of course, made our job much more difficult. It was so costly from a tangible and intangible standpoint that I said, "No more!" No more, that is, until we fix what is wrong.

After a couple of months of research and a lot of soul-searching, we found a "missing link." We were pulling people into an industry of which few had any experience. We were expecting them to succeed without knowing what success really was. In their case, success may have been to simply sell something. Having never sold before, making their first sale is a BIG success—but not enough to establish a successful business. In other words, they had no real feel for what success was or how to get there. Shame on us!

At this point, I began to consider changes that needed to be made in our hiring process that would bring clarity to what was expected and to how the employee would know if they were doing a good or bad job. I developed a single page document that described the duties of the job but also the outcomes that were expected.

Outstanding performers want to be a part of something bigger than themselves—something within reach, but challenging. Phil Jackson, one-time coach of the World Champion Chicago Bulls, wrote in his book, *Sacred Hoops*: *"The most effective way to forge a winning team is to call on the players' need to be part of something larger than themselves."*

People, when they go to work, want to know what is expected of them. They want to be challenged, and they want to be part of something larger than themselves. Marcus Buckingham and Curtis Coffman in their book, *First Break All The Rules,* said,

"One of the top six reasons people leave companies is that they do not know what is expected of them."

Problem solved! The most efficient device capable of addressing that need is the "Performance-Based Job Description" **(PBJD)**. The **PBJD** is always a *one-page document* with three critical pieces: General Duties and Responsibilities, Mission Critical Outcomes (minimum expectations), and Break-Through Outcomes (hoped-for achievements). It is a one-page document because the candidate needs to be able to read it within 2-3 minutes and respond when you ask (in the opening interview), "Did you see anything there you don't think you could do?"

Communicating the vision of what an outstanding performer does and the results that are expected *begins with a vision.* Every job in the organization needs to move the organization closer to that vision. Companies with a powerful vision attract talent. In communicating the corporate vision, take pains to be clear about the destination and the time of arrival. For hiring purposes, the vision and the time of anticipated arrival should be communicated with clarity. Dress it up, spiff it up if you like. Put it on the coffee table and in the reception area. Make it visible to all, but especially to the candidate.

Vision is essential to the
***Performance Based Job Description and* the SHS.**
Clarify your vision and improve your results!

Most job descriptions focus on the steps necessary to please the supervisor. I refer to them as "DO/HAVE" job descriptions. They only sustain stale, uninspired performance and perpetuate mediocrity. The *Performance Based Job Description* provides clarity of expectations to the candidate. Every candidate I have known wants to know what is expected of them.

Where do your employees go to review or clarify what is expected of them ? The job description? The employee procedure manual? Where can they go to clearly define what excellence really means?

The answer: The *Performance Based Job Description.* It is the "plumb line" to which an employee can judge his/her performance. Even more significant, it is the standard by which they will be judged. What is the value of having employees know what is expected of them? Employees say it is priceless. In fact, the Gallup organization referred to in *First Break All The Rules:* "'To know what is expected" is one of the top six things employees felt was necessary to provide an environment where extraordinary results could be obtained on a regular and consistent basis.'"

Most companies design job descriptions that define the steps necessary to succeed—nearly opposite of what is needed. Regardless of the role or position you are filling, it is the organization's job to define the **outcome desired** for the person in that job—**not the steps** to the outcome. In other words, if you are hiring or selecting a person for an entrepreneurial sales role, for instance, instead of outlining the steps to success, clearly define the outcomes required to succeed in that job and ask the employee to develop those expectations. If they need help, help them. But *what you pay them for is their ability to perform the stated requirement.* (See *Appendix* for a PBJD example.)

CHAPTER THREE

PROFILING THE IDEAL CANDIDATE

I was one of those business-owners in the early 80s in Houston that was able to take advantage of the anemic commercial real estate market. I was looking for office space and there was plenty of it—very cheap. I found a building, a new Class A building in a part of the city that I felt was destined for accelerated growth once we got past this difficult economic spot. I wanted to be as certain as possible that I was making the right decision. I had a friend in the insurance business that had been in the same general area for several years. So I thought I would talk with him about his experiences.

I called Cal (my friend) and set a lunch date. I told him I was considering relocating my office in the same general area and just wanted to get his feel for what he thought was going to happen in the future in that part of town.

We met, had a great lunch, and Cal delivered a real "doom and gloom" message. Cal said that he hoped I had not already made a commitment for an office in the area because it was difficult to get people to come this far from the metropolitan area and that he was really suffering because of it. After carefully weighing what Cal had to say and carefully considering the deal I was going to get on the space, I decided to "blow off" what Cal had advised against and to make the move.

It was at this point that I decided—largely due to Cal's influence—that I needed to get clear in my mind the objective of my move and exactly the kind of people I wanted.

"A picture is worth a thousand words." I am not referring to a picture of physical appearance, but rather, a picture of the *competencies* (Talents, Knowledge, and Skills) an ideal candidate must have to achieve the outcomes defined by the **Performance Based Job Description.** When building a team of "Superior Performers," you must have clarity with regard to the competencies that result in the achievement of the outcomes desired. Remember, just one Superior Performer can produce results **seven** times those of a mediocre team member. I have been a business-owner for thirty years, and I have seen the impact of superior performers over and over again. To illustrate my point, the following is a story of how the seeds of the **SHS** sprouted.

Joe was not a particularly impressive guy when he came to me to talk about a position I was filling. The position was one of Agency Manager in Houston, Texas, and I had just begun to build my team that would ultimately become the largest, most successful agency in the state for a number of years. Joe was a Chemist and had been working for the Medical Center as a researcher. He had no real accomplishments to which he could point.

I had just begun to recognize the value of hiring people to a profile rather than people similar to myself. After a number of hires to fill the position and a similar number of failures, I decided that I had to come up with a different plan or give up the idea of sustained superior performance. Facing failure, I decided to do something different in hopes of intervening and stopping the negative impact of low productivity and high turnover.

I decided to list the attributes of a fictitious Manager who would likely produce outstanding results in the position. After a lengthy process of compiling what an ideal candidate should look like, I wrote them out on paper and gradually eliminated all but three things: 1) Knowledge of the industry, 2) Above average communication skills, and 3) An intense commitment to goal setting and achievement.

I interviewed candidates to determine the experience the candidates had in those three competencies. I hired Joe because he was the closest fit to the requirements of the job. Joe not only did well but excelled and led his position for years. Joe was the standard on which the **SHS** was built. *Determine the outcomes you desire and find the people that can get you there!*

I created an **"Ideal Candidate Profile"** (ICP) based on the needs of the job. In other words, determine the knowledge, skills and talents likely to produce superior results in this job. When this is accomplished, as close as possible, build on that.

The **ICP** begins with defining the competencies believed necessary to produce superior results. These competencies come in three classifications: *knowledge, skills, and talents.* The first two—knowledge and skills—can be taught and learned. The third, *Talents,* must be discovered. By far, the most important of the three is Talents. Why? Because, given equal knowledge and skills a person with talent has the potential to out-perform those without it.

So, once you have clearly defined the job and the outcomes desired (**PBJD**), compare your description to those employees you have previously selected (those who have done well in that job, or are doing well in that job, or are supervisors of persons in that job) and brainstorm what competencies and talents are required for superior performance in that specific job.

Begin with the easiest—the **knowledge** necessary to excel. Define the knowledge a candidate needs to excel in this job. A few examples of knowledge that candidates may need are an Engineering degree or Law degree, programming languages, knowledge of the insurance industry, etc. Remember, in brain-storming there are no wrong answers, so get all the ideas out on the table and then identify the essentials followed by the "nice to haves." Make a list and put it on paper. Gradually eliminate all but two or three that are "must haves." These become your knowledge competencies.

Next, use a similar exercise to define the **skills** of an ideal candidate. Skills can best be defined as "knowledge applied." An example of some common skills that might bring value are public speaking, managing people, planning, team-building, presenting, etc. Again, identify two or three essential skills. Then add those that would further enhance the performance of the candidate. I call these skills "nice to haves," because they are not essential, but nice if they come with the package. Reduce them to a list of no more than five.

The third and most important competency is **talent**. Most of us, when we think of talent, think of athletic or musical talent, like Tiger Woods, Pete Sampras, The Beatles, Hank Williams Jr., etc. But *this talent* is the value in people beyond athletic and musical abilities. For instance, engineers have talent, truck drivers have talent, nurses have talent, and shoe salesmen have talent. *Everyone has talent of some kind.* Authors Marcus Buckingham and Curtis Coffman, in their book *"First Break All The Rules,"* defined talent as **"recurring patterns of thoughts, feelings and behavior that can be productively applied."** For our purposes that definition works extremely well.

**To hire talented people, look for
patterns of recurring thoughts, feelings and behavior.**

If you are searching for people that can take your company to the next level, pay close attention to talent. Talent, more than anything else, is capable of propelling an organization to outcomes beyond expectations. (Remember, a Superior Performer can out-perform the mediocre, seven times).

Here are three ways you can build a consensus of talents needed in a particular job:

- **Observation: Observing** the candidate in actual work, which often you do not have the opportunity to do.

75

- **Psychometric Assessments:** A means of measuring what is under the hood, revealing what you can't see.
- **Behavior Based Interviewing:** Asking candidates to tell you about a time when they used the talent for which you are looking, and determine the speed and depth of their reply.

Build your talent requirements for the job through collaboration with high performers that are in the job now, others who have excelled in that job but gone on to other positions, and supervisors of people in that particular job.

There are many descriptions of talents. The *Appendix* has a list of talents that can be used to develop your *"Ideal Candidate Profile,"* or you can—and we recommend—use a psychometric tool to gather others' opinions and compile a composite of all. Regardless of which method you use to identify and designate talents necessary to this job, the focus should always be on those talents likely to produce superior performers. Identify the top three talents that your research has identified as essential to "breakthrough performance." For instance, you may have found that a competitive nature was one thing found as a common thread when you interviewed other top performers in that particular role, and the same is necessary to this position.

At this point you should have the information you need to paint a "life-like" portrait of the competencies of your ideal candidate. Organize that information into a one-page description titled *"Ideal Candidate Profile"* (**ICP**). See that those involved in the selection process have that description with a checklist to record their observations of how well the candidate matches the profile. The "Ideal Candidate Competencies" checklist can be used at various stages of the interview process by the interviewer and observers. You will want to collect and review those surveys after each interview.

CHAPTER FOUR

THE JOB BENCHMARK

Benchmarking has long been an effective tool to measure performance. In this case the term *Job Benchmark* is somewhat misleading. Job Benchmarking is an attempt to define what outcomes are needed to be achieved in a particular job and what a superior performer in that job must look like, to provide an accurate and effective template that describes a superior performer in a given job. It becomes a much easier task to hire superior performers (remember they are seven times more effective than mediocre performers).

The **Job Benchmark** has three parts: the PBJD, the ICP and a *Soft Skills Survey* (SSS). We have already discussed the PBJD and ICP, so, a brief time spent describing the Soft Skills Survey will complete the description.

The **SSS** is what it says—a survey of those who know the job either because they are now in it, have been in it, or have supervised others in it. The survey is about the soft skills necessary to achieve the outcomes described in the PBJD. Participants are asked to identify the talents, values, and behaviors necessary for superior performance in a given job. Each participant is surveyed on-line, and results are combined with other participants to produces a composite definition. The outcome becomes a part of the Job Benchmark.

The Job Benchmark is critical to the selection process. A candidate's talent, values and behavior are measured against the Benchmark to determine Job Fit. A perfect fit would be a candidate with the same talent, values and behavior as those of the Benchmark.

When you complete the Job Benchmark, it is time to prepare the Telephone Interview.

CHAPTER FIVE

THE TELEPHONE INTERVIEW

The Telephone Interview is what I call the "second screen." The "first screen" is always—do they meet the *Ideal Candidate Profile*? The telephone interview is a guardian of your time. It makes little sense to take an hour or two to interview candidates if they don't match the ICP or pass the Telephone Interview.

The Telephone Interview should be short and designed to confirm certain requirements that might not be on a résumé. For instance, determining speaking skills necessary to the job or simply getting a feel of the candidate's ability to connect with people—if that is a requirement of the job.

How should the Telephone Interview be conducted? After you have screened candidates' résumés against the ICP, identify 2-5 of the best matches and *dial and smile*, as they say. Before you dial make sure you have a written script of introduction and the questions you intend to ask.

Some simple rules to prepare for the Telephone Interview are:

- Prepare opening remarks of introduction and purpose (always memorized or read skillfully from a script).

- Include no more than five questions (have them written down with spaces between questions to take notes and record responses.
- Always know the answers you are looking for and upon completion, score their answers against expected answers.
- Take no more than 10 minutes to complete this interview.
- Before you hang up—and only with those you wish to move forward—tell them you will be sending them a brief assessment by email and ask them to complete it.
- Thank them and tell them upon their completion of the assessment you sent them, you will contact them to come in for a face-to-face (Opening Interview).

Some questions you may want to include in the Telephone Interview are:

- Do you have a driver's license?
- What is your driving record like? Any tickets or accidents?
- Do you have a degree?
- Tell me a little about why you are interested in this job.
- Why did you leave your last position?

There are others, but remember this is a short, to the point interview to determine if you want to spend time face-to-face with them in the Opening Interview. Upon completion of the Telephone Interview, invite the successful candidate to take the Emotional Intelligence assessment you will send them via email to be completed before the face-to-face interview.

CHAPTER SIX

THE EMOTIONAL INTELLIGENCE ASSESSMENT

If you look deeply, you will find that emotional intelligence plays a major role in the success of any individual, and as a result, any organization. Likewise, the **absence** of emotional intelligence plays a major role in personal and corporate failures.

To demonstrate, I will share a story of an employee of mine—I will call him Floyd Watson. Floyd was a brilliant guy and had graduated cum laude from the University of Texas. He was a tall, good-looking guy, and he came to me right after graduation. I knew his family. He was intelligent, and wanted to make a lot of money, so I hired him. I didn't think Floyd was really cut out for sales, but I thought, "Who knows?" Ever hired someone in that way? I'll bet you have.

Floyd lasted all of four months. He couldn't run fast enough to get away from a sales job. He was able to learn how to do the tasks necessary to succeed, but he always seemed to approach every task pessimistically. He could not overcome his introverted nature and was unable to communicate in a positive way. My benevolence to hire Floyd cost me about $80,000—if you figure salary, training, and lost opportunity costs. Hiring

Floyd was a lesson I will never forget. Looks and intelligence can get you over the threshold, but once you are in you have to be able to engage, understand, and manage others, and that comes largely through Emotional Intelligence. Floyd had little of the EI required for this job. Floyd did go on to be a very successful engineer at a highly respected research firm.

Emotional Intelligence, what is it?

Simply put, it is Emotional Knowledge—*the ability to recognize your own emotions and those of others and work the two together for the benefit of all.*

Dan Goleman, PhD, said (in his breakthrough book, *Emotional Intelligence*) that "Emotional Intelligence is 92 percent of success on the job."

We, at GMS Talent L P, in Houston Texas, use a simple tool called the EQ—an assessment that measures Emotional Intelligence (EI) quickly and inexpensively.

There is a very important reason I suggest using the EI assessment at this point of the selection of an employee. If the candidate does not have a sufficient level of EI, they will not be successful, no matter what level of experience or intelligence they have. So, don't waste your time on people who do not have Emotional Intelligence; they do not have superior performance potential. The next step is the **Opening Interview**.

Chapter Seven

THE OPENING INTERVIEW

In Houston, 1981, the unemployment rate was so high they were thinking about indexing it, giving it a symbol, and trading it on the stock exchange. The number of work opportunities was at low ebb and the number of people looking for opportunities was at a record high. If you were looking for work in those days, you likely would not find many opportunities. As a result, people used innovative techniques to get the attention of those who had jobs to fill. I remember one instance that taught me a lesson I will never forget.

Before I share the details of that experience, let me give you a little background on my industry and how we hired people. Until the 1980s, if a candidate's body temperature was warm and they could fog a mirror, we hired them. Some in the industry still have their "test mirrors." I, however, had an experience that changed my approach—forever.

I arrived at work one morning all "pumped up." I had scheduled interviews every hour, including lunch hour. I knew I would "nail" the majority of them (sell them on our business opportunity). It would be a good day. Then, Sherry M arrived.

Sherry was a sharp, twenty-something candidate whose résumé looked perfect. She was outgoing and ambitious. I just knew she would be a top agent. It was just something I felt. If you have been hiring for a while, you have had the feeling. So, I turned on the "afterburners" and started selling the opportunity with everything I had.

I was so good I even surprised myself. I knew she could not refuse such a professional "selling job." I had given her every good reason why she should choose my organization. She could not possibly see any more value anywhere else, I thought. I must admit I was a little startled when I put the "close" on her and she pushed back and replied, "I need to "think about it."

"Well," I thought, "she is just young and cautious and needs a little more time." I was right, Sherry M. turned out to be one of the best in the city. The only problem was that she was the "best" for my competitor, who always had a little bit of a "standoffish" attitude toward candidates. I was devastated. "How could she join such an organization?" A few years later, I found out.

I was chairing a committee for an industry organization and Sherry M. was on that committee. We became good friends. One day we were having coffee, and I asked her why she had chosen my competition over me.

I asked, "Do you remember our interview, when you were just considering the building of your own agency?"

"I sure do," she said. "I remember you were masterful. It was all I could do to keep from asking you where to sign."

"Well, why didn't you?" I asked.

"Because it was a big decision for me, and I had made up my mind before I came to talk with you that I would not decide, that day. But what really made me decide to join your competition was your masterful selling job. I thought about our conversation that night and began to wonder, why was he selling me so hard? That prompted me to think that I should investigate the industry a little more before I decided. So I talked with your competition. They did not have what you had, and did not do what you would have done, but they did not know if they *wanted* me on their team. I actually had to sell them on me. I worked so hard at selling them on me that when they bought, I had to accept."

The lesson that Sherry M. taught me was a big one: *When hiring people, remember—you are the buyer!* Don't start selling until you know you want what they have.

That said, here is the layout for the **Opening Interview:**

1. Make sure you are prepared with the PBJD and ICP, the four-color glossy stuff on the company, and the interview questions—don't forget the interview questions!
2. It is your responsibility to make the candidate feel as comfortable as possible.

3. Begin with a welcome and your canned elevator speech. Then ask them to read over the PBJD for the position and to tell you if *they see anything there that they do not believe they could handle. Ask them to initial and date it, and tell them it will become a part of their permanent interview file.*

4. Next, ask the candidate to share the CNN version of their Life Story. Look for leadership roles, goal setting, achievements they are proud of, and other attributes that may be important to this job. This information will also allow you to get to know the candidate better.

5. Then ask specific questions to determine their experiences compared to the General Duties and Responsibilities section of the **PBJD**. Take notes.

6. Ask a closing question like, *"If we are able to meet your financial needs and make an offer, when could you actually begin?"* This is kind of a "trial close." If they are really interested in the job, their answer will be specific, like in *two weeks, or on the first.* If they are not too interested, the answer may be something like, *my mother-in-law is in the hospital and my daughter goes off to Europe when she gets out of school. So, I guess, when my daughter gets back from Europe.*

For the candidate with whom you wish to move forward, the next step is the **TriMetrix Assessment** tool. Get them to take this assessment upon completion of the **Opening Interview**. That way you will have the results, and you can actually match them to the **Job Benchmark** right then and there.

CHAPTER EIGHT

THE TRIMETRIX® ASSESSMENT

Nearly 70 percent of all organizations use assessments in their selection process. Using an assessment to match skills, values, and behaviors of a candidate to the needs of the job is a very important step toward the hiring of Superior Performers. Of course, you can use any type of assessment to match to a benchmark, but we use the TriMetrix because of its simplicity, its guard against gaming the results, and its cost.

There are four very important attributes that drive success on the job. One, we have already talked about—Emotional Intelligence. If they don't have EI, they are not going very far. The other key attributes are *Talent, Values* and *Behavior*. Here is how those three work together to produce superior performers.

Values, formed very early in life, seldom change much. People work to satisfy their values. If their values don't get satisfied, they are unhappy. If they are unhappy, they are "out of here," or worse—unengaged and poor performers. It is important that the candidate's values are satisfied by the job and that the candidate's values match the organization's values.

What we value drives the way we behave. Some may value money, others control, while still others may value living an appropriate lifestyle. These values all drive a specific behavior.

Behavior is all about how we act or behave. Some jobs require us to behave in a supportive way; others require leadership. Behavior is possibly the easiest to observe and to change among those three. Some people are naturally inclined to push toward a goal, while others are more inclined to support people toward a goal. Some are in need of details and support while others want to be left alone, and still others want to talk about feelings and people. How we apply our natural talent is driven by how we behave.

Talent, or innate abilities, is driven by the way we behave. Values, Behavior, and Talent are what I call "The Triple Threat." All are measured by the TriMetrix® assessment tool.

Matching the personal competencies against the needs of the job allows us to better gage **Job-Fit**. The right person in the wrong job is never a good situation.

Chapter Nine

THE SELECTION INTERVIEW

We are coming down to the wire. Thus far the candidate/candidates have passed the ICP screen, Telephone Interview screen, Emotional Intelligence screen, Opening Interview screen, TriMetrix/Job Benchmark screen, and now we are at the final screening—**The Selection Interview.**

The *Selection Interview* is tied to the **Job Benchmark.** This is the final interview, and it is designed to confirm whether or not the candidate actually uses their "Talents." The TriMetrix assessment has already told us the capacity the candidate has to perform in the job. Please remember that assessments don't tell you if a candidate is actually using the talent they have; assessments only tell you the capacity the candidate has. They may not be using their talent at all, or they may be deficient but are performing in an excellent manner because they have built skills around a weakness that allows them to perform in a superior manner regardless of their capacity.

The Job Benchmark will contain a series of 7 talents, 2 values, and 2 behaviors. Listed here are examples of possible competencies:

Talents (7)

- Self-Management
- Resiliency
- Self-Starting
- Personal Accountability
- Goal Achievement
- Interpersonal Skills
- Results Orientation

Values (2)

- Utilitarian
- Individualistic

Behaviors (2)

- Urgency
- Frequent Interaction with Others

The TriMetrix ranks a candidate's talents, hierarchically, from their strongest to their weakest. A quick check for a match-up of the candidate's top talents against those of the Job Benchmark will determine Job Fit.

If the assessment tells you capacity only, how do you determine if the candidate actually uses their talent? Two ways: by observing them in action or by the interview. Since we can seldom observe others in action, the interview is a very valuable tool.

In the *Selection Interview,* questions are prepared around the eleven attributes of the benchmark. And here is a big secret— you can accurately determine if a person is using their talent by crafting behavior style questions around the talents you are looking for and measuring the speed and depth of the answers the person gives. Here's the thought behind that:

If a person uses a talent frequently, they will have lots of stories about their use and they will have top of mind recall, with a lot of depth.

If, on the other hand, you ask a question and the candidate cannot give you a quick response or gives one that seems contrived, it is likely that they are not using their talent. Here are some examples of Behavioral Style questions based on the seven talents mentioned above:

1. Tell us about a time when you were challenged beyond your natural ability. What did you do? What was the outcome?
2. When was the last time someone in authority said "no" to you? How did you feel? What did you do?
3. Tell me about a time you were left to complete a big project on your own. How did you motivate yourself to get started every day?
4. When was the last time you failed at something important? Whose fault was it? What did you do?
5. What are your most important goals for the next 12 months and some of the actions steps you will take to achieve them?

6. How would you rate your interpersonal skills on a scale of 1-10? Why?
7. What is your current most important goal and what steps will you take to achieve it?

You should be getting the idea.

At the end of the Selection Interview ask another trial-closing question such as, *"I really like what I see here and I may have to work to meet your needs, but if I did, when would you be able to begin?"* If they are specific, they are interested in your company and the job. If they are not specific, they are not really interested in the job.

Inform them that they will hear from you within seven working days. Ask if they have any questions. Answer them and say Goodbye!

CHAPTER TEN

JOB FIT AND JOB OFFER

We are on the five yard-line—1st and goal. Let's not fumble now. The very important question is, *"Does this person fit the needs of the job?"* We should know by now. Comparing the results of the three interviews, two assessments and matching the knowledge, experience and skills of the candidate to the Job Benchmark should indicate whether or not there is a good fit.

Hopefully, you have more than one candidate, so you can compare results and pick the one you like the best among those who fit. You should move in a deliberate and timely manner. Do not wait for anything once you have made your evaluation. Many superior performers are lost in this last step because an organization can't make up their mind. An offer letter or regret should go out in no less than three working days from the end of the Selection Interview.

The offer letter should contain job specifics, expiration date, written request to reply and a desired start date. Even the very best hire cannot survive if there is not a track to run on.

For information on the critical On-Boarding step, refer to the book:

THE TARGET-The Secret to Superior Performance, by Stephen J. Blakesley, published by Tate Publishing and available at this website: **www.gmstalent.com.**

APPENDIX

THE STRATEGIC HIRING SYSTEM©

Performance Based Job Description
(Example Only)

General Duties and Responsibilities:

Position: Agent Associates

Reports To:

➤ Meets or exceeds production goals.

➤ Actively builds network with mortgage companies and auto dealers.

➤ Actively pursues expanded knowledge of insurance and sales.

Dazzles the customer. Meets all their needs and then some.

➤ Completes the "90 Plan."

➤ Attends all training.

➤ Attends and participates in Agency Sales meetings.

➤ Learns and understands products; meets all underwriting standards.

➤ Is accountable to Agency Manager.

➤ Actively recruits and refers other potential Agency producers.

Mission Critical Outcomes:

> ➤ Meets seasonally adjusted Productions standards of $250,000 annually.
>
> ➤ Meets all compliance and underwriting standards within 90 days of hire and thereafter.
>
> ➤ Develops Agent Associate Business Plan, including goals and actions to achieve goals.
>
> ➤ Completes Goal Planning Worksheet within 90 days of hire.

Break Through Outcomes:

> ➤ Consistently exceeds minimum Productions Standards.
>
> ➤ Consistently recognized among the top 5 producers after 90 days of hire.

Ideal Candidate Profile *(Example Only)*

Position:
Reports To:
IDEAL Knowledge:
4-year college degree from an accredited college or university.
IDEAL Experience:
4 years in sales with experience on commission only.
IDEAL Skills:
Expert level MS Office, Multilingual - English and Spanish.
IDEAL Emotional Intelligence:
Customer Focus, Personal Accountability, Resiliency, Goal Achievement , Self-Management, Diplomacy & Tact, Results Orientation
IDEAL Values:
Utilitarian/Economic, Traditional/Regulatory, Individualistic/Political
IDEAL Behavior:
Frequent Interaction w/Others, Versatility, Customer Oriented
IDEAL Work Strategies:
Networking, Initiative, Show and Tell, Self-Management, Teamwork
IDEAL Emotional Quotient Skills:
Meets or exceeds national mean in Self Awareness, Self-Regulation, Empathy, and Social Skills. Exceeds the mean in Motivation.

ESSENTIAL Knowledge:
HS Diploma.

ESSENTIAL Experience:
2 years in sales of intangibles.

ESSENTIAL Skills:
Intermediate level MS Office, Reads, writes, and speaks the English language very well.

ESSENTIAL Emotional Intelligence :
Customer Focus, Personal Accountability, Resiliency, Goal Achievement , Self-Management

ESSENTIAL Values:
Utilitarian/Economic, Traditional/Regulatory, Individualistic/Political

ESSENTIAL Behavior:
Frequent Interaction w/Others, Versatility, Customer Oriented

ESSENTIAL Work Strategies:
Networking, Initiative, Show and Tell, Self-Management, Teamwork

ESSENTIAL Emotional Quotient Skills:
Meets or exceeds national mean in Self Awareness, Self-Regulation, Empathy, and Social Skills. Exceeds the mean in Motivation.

Interview Examples

The Telephone Interview *(example only)*

Preparation: Clear your desk review the *Performance Based Job Description, Ideal Candidate Profile, and Soft Skills survey.* Review the names and résumés of those you wish to call. Locate your Opening Interview Questions and Scoring System in front of you. Have a pen or pencil handy to take notes. Smile and Dial.

Opening Remarks: *Mr./Ms.* _____ *this is* _____ *(name and title) with* **XYZ COMPANY.** *We are an organization that provides insurance and financial services customized to fit your needs. In particular, we are seeking an outstanding individual to fill a* **Managing Agent** *position. May I ask you a few questions?*

1.	Do you have a 4-year college degree or equivalent?
ANS	

2.	Have you had any experience selling on a commission only basis?
ANS	

3.	Have you supervised sales people for a period of at least a year?
ANS	

4.	Do you know your credit rating?

ANS	
5.	What is it that appeals to you about this job?
ANS	

	Score
Award 20 points for every positive answer:	

Opening Interview Date & Time Set: _____

Interviewer: _____ Date of Interview: _____

The Opening Interview *(Example only)*

Part I: Life Journey

Opening: *"Mr./Ms. _____, the purpose of our time together today is to get to know one another a little better. To begin, let me give you a brief overview of* **XYZ COMPANY.** *Because of our expertise and commitment to excellence, we are experiencing astonishing growth. Because of that growth, we are seeking Superior Performers to help us continue expansion. We are not looking for people that can simply do the job, but rather for people that will exceed our expectations. In other words—"Game Breakers."*

"Now that I have shared a little about **XYZ COMPANY,** *please give me a brief description of your life's journey from grade school to today. Please tell me about your victories and your defeats. I'll be taking a few notes so please be specific about those events that you feel are important to you and me."*

1.	Look for any leadership roles.
ANS =	
2.	Look for any mentioned achievements.
ANS =	
3.	Listen for indications of goal setting.

4.	Listen for management experience.
ANS =	
5.	Listen for any sales achievements.
ANS =	
	Scoring: Award 20 points for each of the adequate answer, O points for each inadequate answer.

The Opening Interview *(Example only)*

Part II: Discovery
General Duties and Responsibilities

"Thank you for sharing that information. Now if it is all right with you I would like to ask a few questions."

1.	If you were selected for this position, tell me how you would market and promote your agency products. (Look for knowledge of the power of networking within the mortgage and auto industries.)

ANS=

2.	When a customer complains, what do you do? (Look for take ownership until the problem is resolved.)

ANS=

3.	Tell me about how you work to create an environment where your people can be the best they can be. (Look for an understanding that they are responsible for creating that environment and what that environment would look like.)

ANS=

4.	What are your financial goals for the next year, 3 years? (Make sure they have some specific financial goals.)

ANS=

5.	Tell me about your latest recruiting experience. (Look for knowledge of the challenges and the ability to overcome challenges.)

ANS=

6.	Tell me about your experience in, and responsibility for, office operations. (Look for knowledge of costs, leases, and other factors that impact profits.)
ANS=	

7.	What is your office communication policy? (Look for making sure everyone understands the important factors and communication of them in an effective way.)
ANS=	

8.	What is your philosophy on sales meetings? (Look for knowledge of their value and an effort to learn and keep up to date.)
ANS=	

9.	How do you feel about the need for and value of reporting results. (Look for recognition of the accountability value of reporting.)
ANS=	

10.	Tell me about your most successful sales experiences? Sales Management Expenses? (Look for aggressive prospecting, planning, closing, and follow-up knowledge.)
ANS=	

Scoring: Award 20 points for each answer that is acceptable, in your judgment. Award 0 points for each inadequate answer.

The Selection Interview *(Example only)*

The purpose of this interview is to determine if the candidate has the soft skills necessary to excel in the job. (Look for speed of response and depth of response.)

1	When it is important for you to accomplish a certain goal and you fail, generally, what is the reason. (Look for recognition that he/she is responsible for own actions no matter the circumstances)

ANS=

2	Tell me what you believe some of the most important traits of a leader might be and why you think so. (Look for an understanding that leaders need to be visionaries, they need to be trustworthy, honest, and competent in their field)

ANS=

3	When you begin a new project, how do you organize your time, energy, and focus? (Look for an understanding that what you pay attention to (focus on) usually gets done and that they not only understand but have actually applied those principles)

ANS=

4	Tell me about your philosophy regarding a leader's responsibility to the people who work for him/her. (Look for an understanding that the leader's responsibility is to create an environment where people can be the best they can be.)

ANS=

5	Should you be selected for this position what are some of the first things you would be doing? (Look for planning and goal setting along with building their network)

ANS=

6	What are some of the most effective efforts, used by you, to develop your network? (Look for regular and consistent new contacts, a clear understanding of the type of network needed, and how to find them, and develop them)

ANS=

7	When it is important for you to convince others to accept your plan or follow you, how do you approach the need to influence them to accept your view? Tell me about a time when it was necessary for you to do so and how it came out. (Look for a quick response and a believable story of how they influenced others to their position.)

ANS=

8	Think back over the people you have worked with and tell me about someone you know that consistently displayed unusual initiative. On a scale of 1- 10, w/10 = best, how would you rate their initiative? (Wait for answer then ask the following.) Now, how would you rate your initiative and why? (Look for 7 or better and clear understanding that initiative involves self-starting, persistence, and exceptional commitment to getting the job done.)

ANS=

9	Tell me about the books you have recently read and what you learned? (Look for an under-standing that leaders must develop their skills and the skills of others and that reading is one source of information and inspiration)

ANS=

10 Should you be selected for this job, what is the most important thing you would hope to get from it? (Look for money, opportunity to achieve their goals, and personal satisfaction)

ANS=

Scoring: Award 20 points for each answer that is adequate, in your judgment. Award 0 points for each inadequate answer.

Stephen J. Blakesley

PART THREE

THE MAGNIFICENT SEVEN

~Seven Habits of Superior Performers~

Stephen J. Blakesley

FORWARD

If you are one of many organizations that believed you could build a high performing team simply by hiring only the *"brightest and best,"* you probably know by now that you were mistaken.

Robert Kelley, author of *How to be a Star at Work,* spent five years at the once prestigious Bell Labs trying to find out why that strategy did not produce higher performing people in greater numbers. Bell Labs hired nothing but the *brightest and the best* for many years in the late 80s and early 90s, yet most of the hires ended with a mediocre rating. In fact, almost 80 percent of their hires were rated "mediocre performers" by their peers. What a disappointment and a waste of money.

So what was missing among these talented and intelligent people? Why were so few considered superior performers? Part Three of this book reveals the reasons and addresses action to be taken within your organization to increase the percentage of superior or high performing people.

Stephen J. Blakesley

Prologue

Why is the subject of performance important enough to devote time and effort to get better at it?

Performance, as defined by Webster's, is *the act or process of performing.* In the workplace it is about execution, doing, achievement and attainment. *Superior Performance* is all of that, but at a higher level. We are not born superior performers. Some people never become superior performers, but those who do can change the world. If you believe that and want to leave the world better than you found it, the time you devote to reading this section of the book will bring you closer to that goal.

Recently, in a SONY stockholder's meeting, a presentation was made to draw attention to the world of today and tomorrow. The presenter made the following points that I profoundly believe define the world we live in—and the world in which we will soon live:

- In a very short time, China will be the largest English-speaking nation in the world.

- If you are just graduating from college, or you have children who are, they will have 14 jobs before they are 38 years old.
- The top 25 percent of India's most intelligent is a greater number than the entire population of the United States

All of that translates into more competition, accelerating change, and a growing need to get better if you want to excel. Simply living and working in the United States will not be enough.

INTRODUCTION

The study of high-performers, in the crucible of today's business environment, has given us a clear understanding of what it is that separates the mediocre performer from the superior.

The simplest and clearest lessons to be learned boils down to just two things:

1. Intelligence is not necessarily an indicator of future performance in the workplace.
2. Superior performers have very specific work habits that are responsible for their performance.

This section of the book is about those very specific habits of *superior performers*. It is about what I call **The *Magnificent Seven—seven work habits that pave the road to superior performance.***

What are the seven habits that distinguish the mediocre from the superior?

- **Initiative**: Learning how to work in places unexpected and going beyond expectations

- **Self-Management:** Being able to manage every aspect of your life, regardless of whether it is personal or business. Managing effort as well as time. Controlling emotions and leveraging strengths.
- **Networking:** Many times more important now than in the 90s. Developing a network before you need them. It is not only about strong connections but about weak ones as well. It is about developing a web of people that can get you what you want.
- **Leadership:** Knowing that the small 'ℓ' in leadership is far more important within the organization than the big "L." Knowing how to lead from within a workgroup or team is the all-important small 'ℓ'.
- **Followership:** Understanding that everyone follows some-one. Being able to set aside your ego to be the best in a supportive role.
- **Perspective:** A unique ability to see how your job con-tributes to the organization's success. Understanding how you fit into the big picture.
- **Teamwork:** Understanding the value and purpose of the team. Matching your talents with the needs of the team. Recognizing and supporting others in their efforts to achieve a common goal.

Through the next several pages are some of the most important and valuable strategies for advancing productivity you will ever read. Take it slow and absorb it deeply, not only for your personal use, but also to share with others so they, too, might become all they can be.

CHAPTER ONE

INITIATIVE—*A FIRST STEP*

Possibly, one of the best examples of *Initiative* and how it can impact success is the story of Larry Bird. Larry Bird was both an all-time top player *and* coach in the NBA. Bird had a remarkable career (13 years, all as a Boston Celtic). He qualified for the All-Star team in all but one of those years. He was the last player to win Rookie of the Year and Player of the Year in the same season (1979-1980). He was designated MVP in the NBA three years in a row and helped lead his team to three consecutive NBA championships in 1981-82, 1983-84, and 1985-86.

Bird retired in 1992, but the story of his accomplishments doesn't stop there. He was one of the very few NBA players to become a successful coach. In 1997 he became the coach of the Indiana Pacers and won Coach of the Year award—making him the only person to have ever won both MVP and Coach of the Year in the history of the NBA.

In his autobiography, *Drive: The Story of My Life*, he describes a drive to keep growing, no matter what the obstacles. He regularly and consistently stepped out, risking all to get better.

It is that determination, that self-commitment I am calling *Initiative*. It is "working in the white spaces" of your job description. *Initiative* is taking the first step to be better, regardless of what you have done in the past.

Initiative is about a willingness to take on risk. It is about taking the first step without a cattle prod to your butt. It is about drive, dash, snap, punch, zing and pizzazz. Possibly one of the most exciting discoveries you and I will ever make is when we discover those with *Initiative*—within our own family, organization, or even ourselves.

Russell Conwell, a Baptist minister, delivered a speech that was later to become a book. The title of the speech and the book is *Acres of Diamonds*. It is about the diamonds in our own back yard. He delivered this speech over 6000 times in the 1890s and nearly all of the proceeds went to establish what we now know as Temple University.

This book, *Acres of Diamonds*, has become a classic and is about an Arab farmer who sold his land and belongings to search for diamonds. He spent his life and wealth doing so, unsuccessfully, while those to whom he sold his very own farm discovered the richest diamond mine in the world—in what was once his own back yard.

Such is the case in many families and organizations. We spend our time and our wealth looking for something that is right "under our noses." Many organizations and families are filled with people demonstrating one of the foundational attributes of superior performers—*Initiative*.

One of the most vivid examples of latent *initiative* is the story of Wilma Rudolf—once known as the fastest woman in the world. She was born prematurely, weighing 4.5 pounds. She was the youngest of 21 brothers and sisters and was afflicted with polio at an early age. Her legs were twisted, and she wore heavy braces just to be able to walk. But she was not deterred by her difference. While her mother worked, Wilma had a routine she was to follow to exercise her legs, but she always did more than was expected. She was supposed to walk with her braces on for at least an hour a day, but she actually took the braces off against her mother's adamant instructions and walked around the house as many times as she could. She was determined to be like the other kids. She continued to walk and exercise, in secret, and against her mother's wishes. Her family drove her regularly from Clarksville to Nashville for treatment of her twisted legs, and Wilma kept asking the doctor when she could walk without the braces. Finally, the doctor gave in and said, "Okay." She could take them off, but only for brief periods at first. That was all Wilma needed to hear—the braces never touched her legs again.

Wilma went on to win three gold medals in the 1960 Olympics. The French called her the "La Pearle Noire" (the Black Pearl) and the Italians tagged her "La Gazelle Negra" (the Black Gazelle). In her own country she was known as "The Tornado," and she was certainly the most famous among the famous Tennessee State "Tigerbelles,"a name coined for the TSU women's Track and Field participants. Had Wilma not displayed the *Initiative* to remove the braces and push herself to be "like other kids" she may never have become "La Pearle Noire" and women's Track and Field gold medal winner.

So, if you want to be a superior performer, perhaps it begins with *Initiative*—do something about it! Survey your strengths, set some goals, and begin!

CHAPTER TWO

SELF MANAGEMENT—*CHARACTERISTICS OF A SUPERIOR PERFORMER*

Self-management is more than just managing time and emotions—it begins with Self-Discovery. But before self-discovery, we must at least have a sense of what we *can* discover about ourselves. What characteristics, what attributes impact performance? Then the question is how can these attributes be managed to benefit me and/or the organization?

Characteristics and attributes
When you think about performance, many factors come into play:

- It is not only the *attributes of the individual*, but also the environment in which the individual performs that impacts performance.
- It is not just about *attributes that impact the individual*; it is about how those attributes impact others, as well.

No man or woman stands alone. Our attitudes and attributes impact those around us and their performance as well as ours.

Self-management is complex and difficult. It doesn't happen by accident.

Some of the characteristics that are under the management umbrella are one's actions and attitudes. Some of these characteristics, for instance, include attitude, moods, emotions, organizational savvy, focus, speech, self-image, self-esteem, and self-confidence. If anyone were to do an exceptional job at managing all of these six, they would be a superior performer.

A great example of how moods, for instance, impact performance of both yourself and others, would be to visualize just one drive to work over the last couple of weeks.

If you have any distance to drive, most likely you have found yourself in traffic—oftentimes unexpected traffic. Occasionally, you might have encountered a driver with less intelligence, awareness, and compassion than you, who rudely "cut you off" and nearly caused an accident. You utter a few expletives and offer an obscene hand gesture or two and congratulate yourself on your skill at being able to avoid an accident. Still, the whole thing aggravates you and makes you a little angry.

Still in an aggravated mood when you arrive at work, you walk through the door showing less than your usual personality, and you don't even speak to the receptionist—who is always friendly. You march down the hall to your office, passing several co-workers along the way, and you don't speak to them, either.

Stop right there! Each one of those people you have encountered is wondering what's wrong with him or what did they do to you to deserve such rudeness. Those thoughts linger on with them and certainly affect their performance, some more than others. Also, we haven't even begun to analyze what your aggravated mood will do to your performance that day.

Focus and application

Focus and application requires "effort." Being able to manage "effort" is all about developing one's focus and application. When I ask people, "What are your strengths?" I often get the "deer-in-the-headlights" look and a response like, "I don't know; I haven't really thought about it." Superior performance does require thinking about it! In fact, thinking about it may be the most effective thing you can do to achieve superior performance. There is a wealth of talent that goes to waste because people do not make the effort to think about using their talents as effectively as they can.

Developing strategies to discover our talents is like finding the keys to your car. Once you have found them, you can get going. Talent without application is worthless.

Charlton Heston and Self-management

An example of the value and power of *self-management* can be found in the life of actor Charlton Heston. Heston, the actor that became Moses on the screen in the Ten Commandments, and gave us one of the most memorable movie racing scenes ever in Ben Hur, was a big believer in the power of self-management. It is no wonder that he played many great men throughout his career. Taking every opportunity to refine his acting skills as a young man, he became well grounded in self-management.

He went to Northwestern University on scholarship where he proved himself as an actor and developed the confidence that would propel him to fame and fortune. In an interview he said, "Almost overnight, I managed to find the confidence that has never left me. Understand nothing had really happened—except inside my head. Almost overnight, I was certain I would get any part for which I read. You have no idea how crucial this is."

Managing his confidence level was important, but managing his knowledge through the rigorous research he did to prepare for every part was yet another way he managed the outcome of managing self. When he was being considered for the part of Moses, he spent months reading for the part, studying the history and environment of the times. His preparation not only gave him material to discuss with director DeMille, he also understood the grandeur of the project. Heston learned to ignore the critics and focus on what he could do to get better. One of his favorite quotes was from Teddy Roosevelt: "It is not the critic who counts, not the man who points out where the strong stumbled.......the credit belongs to the one that is in the arena, whose face is marred by dust, sweat and blood of effort, who falls and rises again and again."

Self-management has many facets: self-awareness, self-confidence, self-image, time and effort management, etc.

Making the effort to improve in any of these areas
Has a positive impact on performance.

CHAPTER THREE

MAKING YOUR WORLD SMALLER

Knowing what you know is good but *knowing what you don't know is even better*. Before you can get better you must, at least, know what you don't know so you can decide what you want to learn. Twenty-five years ago, surveys said people had about 75 percent of the knowledge necessary to do their jobs. In their heads, they needed to ask for help only about one-fourth of the time. Today, depending upon which source you use, the need to seek outside help has risen rapidly. Among those surveyed in the last 3 years, the need to find help from sources outside one's self has climbed from 25 percent to nearly 75 percent—*a full 50 point swing*.

Experts tell us the knowledge-generation is accelerating. According to some, the cumulative knowledge of the world is doubling every two days. Therefore, the day after tomorrow you will need to know twice as much as you did today—just to do your job. I know that sounds ridiculous, but it is becoming more and more difficult to stay on top of the knowledge needed to excel in your work. Superior performers recognize this fact. They not only know it, but they act on it by building *knowledge networks* before they need them.

There has been much study of networks, of how they work and benefit people involved in them. A body of knowledge known as *Six Degrees of Separation* proposes that you or I are no more than six intermediaries from what would be necessary to connect us with anyone in the world. For those of you who take this value lightly, let me share with you a couple of personal experiences that are absolutely remarkable.

Part of what I do is recruiting, and a few months back a client called with a job order. The order was not the typical order; it went something like this, *"We want to hire someone experienced in the manufacturing of FBICs (Flexible Intermediate Bulk Containers), to work in Saudi Arabia, at an unknown location, for an unknown employer, for an unlimited amount of time."* Just the uncertainty of location, employer and length of job might pose problems for some candidates, however, there is more. T*he candidate must live in Turkey or Saudi and speak either English and Chinese or English and Turkish.* I know it seems like a strange combination, and I wondered about it, too (I will address it for you later). *Oh yes, they required the hire be made within 30 days*

First, let me state that I am really good at what I do, but I knew this was going to be a challenge—a big one! I did not know anything about FBICs, much less know anyone living in Turkey or Saudi who spoke either of those languages. What a challenge!

Here is how I successfully identified several candidates for our client in less than two weeks. I contacted a friend who was in the logistic business and asked for the name of industry associations that might deal with FBICs and their manufacturers. I then began calling people on the membership list asking if they knew anyone in the FBIC business in Turkey. Very early in the calling, I spoke with an individual in Lafayette, Louisiana who had an engineer friend in Turkey that might help. He gave me his contact information and I called him. He knew two candidates in the FBIC business who also knew four more and from those six candidates we made the hire. Networking with people who have a sphere of knowledge beyond my own got the job done.

There is just one more example that I will tell you about here of how Networking pays off. As I told you earlier, we are recruiters and good at what we do. Some even say we are *superior performers* in that space. Just a few weeks ago, a client came to us with a job order and a presumed outcome. He said, "I doubt if you can help us because the time is limited and the target is so small, but please try."

Here was the need: a chemical engineer, with experience in polypropylene manufacturing and the use of a particular catalyst—no other combination would work. Being the optimist that I am, I accepted the job order and went to work.

It did not take me long to find out that I had possibly bitten off more than I could chew. After my research, I found that there may be only six to twelve people in the world with that experience. In two days we had identified two of the possible twelve people in the world and found one—right here in Houston. The client hired him and consummated his contract, worth many thousands, possibly millions of dollars.

How did we do it? Through a network that was laid ahead of time. Through our LinkedIn affiliation, we put out the word of our needs and within four days we had the two candidates mentioned earlier. That network spread from Houston, Texas to one of twelve people in the world with the needed experience and expertise.

"Building a Professional Network is a foundation piece to being a superior performer."

CHAPTER FOUR

LEADERSHIP—*BEING A LEADER WHEN YOU ARE NOT THE LEADER*

If EQ is not present there will be no followers, and without followers there are no leaders.

When most of us think of leadership we think of great leaders we have known or read about, like Eisenhower, Churchill, Reagan, Welch, Disney, etc. Those leaders were and are important, but the most important leaders are those that get no recognition and are rarely heard about—those who lead even though they are not the leader. There are far more leaders, with a small "l" than those mentioned above. I might even go as far as saying the big "L" leaders get more recognition but are not as important.

Learning the make-up of a small "ℓ" leader is the beginning of becoming one. I do believe that leaders of the small ℓ type are made, not born. Assuming I am correct in that statement, you might ask, "What are the attributes of a small ℓ leader?" The answer is complex and not comprehensive, but it gives us a place to begin if we are interested in developing ourselves or others as small ℓ leaders.

Small "*ℓ*" leadership begins with Emotional Intelligence (EQ). I do not believe that you can lead others, over a sustainable period, without a high level of EQ. The ability of understanding your own emotions and the emotions of others is essential to leadership. Being able to use your own emotions to guide the emotions of others is a learned skill—but an essential one to leadership. It makes no difference what other leadership skills you may have. If you do not have a high level of EQ, you are like a fiddle without a bow or a car without a key.

James Kouzes, the Dean's Executive Professor of Leadership, Santa Clara University, and Barry Posner, PhD, Dean of the School of Business at Santa Clara University, have studied leadership around the world for over 20 years in search of aspiring leaders and managers who develop leaders. Each year they compiled a list of the most admired qualities of leaders. The top four traits admired by others which appear year after year, are:

- Honesty
- Forward-Looking
- Inspiring
- Competent

It is my belief that if one works to build those four qualities and has a high level of EQ, they will find themselves in the position of leadership whether they want it or not. Successful leadership depends greatly upon how these qualities are put to use.

Here are five steps to successful application of leadership attributes and skills:

- **Walk the talk**—be known for doing what you say you will do.
- **See the glass as half-full**—and get others to agree.
- **Be willing to challenge the process**—step out. Take cal-culated risks to challenge the status quo.
- **Grease the track for others**—help your peers get a "leg up."
- **Practice "High Touch"**—make sure your touch reflects your talk. Be decent to others.

Walking the Talk

I recently hired an IT type of guy to do some work on my website. I hired him "sight unseen" on the strength of a referral from a colleague. This guy has you pay up front then gives you an estimate on a completion date. He does not want you to call him; he communicates by e-mail only. When he misses the completion date he does not respond to inquiries until at least three days have passed. He then tells you the work will be completed tomorrow, and—you guessed it—tomorrow comes and goes and the work is still not done.

Obviously, this is a customer service problem, not a leadership problem, but it is a great example of someone who does not "walk the talk." Be a person that people champion as someone who always does what they say they are going to do.

See the Glass Half-Full

Be an optimist—people are attracted to optimists like steel to a magnet. Look beyond today, work to see what others cannot see. Be rationally optimistic. You have history on your side.

Be Willing to Challenge the Process

There will always be those who say, "That's the way we have always done it." While the way things have always been done *may* be the best way, sometimes it is *not*. If no one ever challenges, nothing changes. Every day at work, or as you live your life, should be a day you can say you "pushed the envelope." You challenged the system.

Grease the Track for Others

Everyone can use a little help now and then. You be the one who does the helping. Watch for opportunities to help someone on your team reach an important goal. Look for opportunities to impact results for someone else.

Practice "High Touch"

Always make sure your touch mimics your talk. One of the best stories exemplifying this practice is told by Max DePree, once chairman of Hermann Miller, the office furniture leader.

Max tells the story about his granddaughter, Zoe. Zoe was born eight weeks premature to his daughter and son-in-law—who had already walked away from the marriage. Zoe weighed only a pound–and-a-half. She could be held in the palm of your hand and was given little hope of survival. Max, wanting to help, asked the neo-natal nurse in charge what was the best thing he could do to impact the chances of Zoe's survival.

She said to him, "Come to the hospital every day, pick her up in your hand and hold her for twenty minutes, all the time whispering to her that you love her, and don't forget to take your little finger and rub her arms and legs while you are telling her you love her. That way she can connect your talk with your touch and the talk is more meaningful to her." Wow! What a lesson! To make your talk meaningful, reach out and touch someone.

So, the small "l" leadership begins with *Emotional Intelligence*, is enhanced by *honesty*, your desire to *look forward* instead of back, your ability to *inspire*, communicate, and get buy-in, and finally, your technical competency. Then you need a strategy to deliver those qualities, and that strategy is the Five-Step Plan laid out above: Walk the talk, be optimistic, challenge the process, help others and be a "High Touch" person.

CHAPTER FIVE

FOLLOWSHIP—*HOW TO LEAD IN ASSISTS*

Followers do most of the work and are responsible for achieving the goals.

Chances are you did not grow up dreaming of being a great follower. That is not the American way, or is it? American corporations spend billions each year on finding, or trying to find, leaders. They spend billions developing the ones they have found and the ones they thought were leaders—but turned out differently. Then they spend billions more trying to keep the ones they found and "developed."

You could put all the money corporate America has spent on *followership* in one "small box." Yet, we all know that it is the followers that do most of the work and are responsible for achieving the goals of an organization. We know a lot about leadership but much less about *followership*. Think about it for a moment.

There would be no leaders if there were no followers. Are all followers the same? Robert Kelly doesn't think so. In his article for the Harvard Business Review titled, *In Praise of Followers,* he identifies five different follower styles based on two dimensions: How they think—do they think for themselves, or do they look to the leader to do their thinking—and their level of engagement? Do they exhibit high energy in a positive way or low energy in a negative way?

Based on the evaluation of these two dimensions he determined the following five styles of followership:

Sheep: These are the passive, low energy followers that look to the leader for their thinking. These are people who need motivation externally, regardless of whether it is fear or reward. They are not likely to do much without being told what to do.

Yes People: These followers have a positive attitude but still look to the leader for their thinking. These are the people who do what they are told, then come back asking *what do you want me to do next?* Yes people look at following as *doing*. It is the boss's job to do the thinking.

The Alienated: These followers are independent thinkers but tend to think negatively. They are the ones who always have reasons why it won't work. Whenever the organization tries to move forward, they are the ones saying, "It won't work." Or, "We have never done it that way."

The Pragmatics: These are the people who wait to see which direction the wind is blowing, then jump on board. They are chameleons and change directions whenever it seems politically correct.

The Stars: These followers are independent thinkers with positive energy. They accept the leader's lead but always check it against their own evaluation of soundness. They are not fearful of challenging decisions but do so in a manner that is respectful of the leader's position. They are typically identified as "small ℓ" leaders, or "leaders in waiting."

Star Performer Model

Developed by Dr. Robert Kelley

Within your group, see if you can identify members of these four groups and decide which best fits you.

Leaders / Followers

So, what is the best way to view this whole idea of followership? My thoughts are that followers and leaders have a *reciprocal relationship with a common purpose.* One cannot exist without the other. Every leader was a follower at one time or other. You can't have followers without leaders and vice versa. But the glue that holds the two together is the *common purpose*.

What common purpose is there that promulgates leaders and followers? The answer is *a common objective*, a goal that benefits both and an understanding that *all* of us can be better than *one* of us. If your organization does not have a *Followership* training program, please consider one. We can help.

Possibly, one of the greatest examples of how great followers make great leaders is the story of Dwight David Eisenhower. Eisenhower was a five star general in the United States Army, and the 34th President of the United States of America. But he was not always in a leadership role.

Eisenhower was born in Dennison, Texas. He was the third born of seven brothers (follower). He graduated from the United States Military Academy at West Point in 1915. From there he began his followership. In WW I, he trained tank crews but never saw battle.

After the war, he became the Executive Assistant (follower) to General Fox Connor in the Panama Canal Zone. Later he served as Executive Officer to General George V. Mosely, then Secretary of War. After that he was the Chief Military Aide to General George MacArthur, then Army Chief of Staff. All this time following and learning how to be a good follower. Just before WW II he held a series of staff positions where he was a follower.

During WW II, he again served as a follower and aide to Chief of Staff General George C. Marshall. Not until 1942 was Eisenhower appointed to a true leadership role, Commanding General of the European Theater of Operations. In 1944, he became the Supreme Allied Commander and began leading those he once followed.

Not without the journeyman experience in following would Eisenhower ever have emerged as one of the greatest leaders of our times. Great Followers make Great Leaders!

Stephen J. Blakesley

CHAPTER SIX

TEAMWORK—*SOME OF US*
ARE BETTER THAN ONE OF US

In nearly every case, teams are better than individuals. Multiple talents, viewpoints, experiences and resources bring a stunning array of values to the table. No individual has the diversity or richness of a team. But, learning to work with others is often challenging. Yet, the team concept has great value. Possibly one of the best examples of teamwork, in recent times, is that of W. L. Gore and Associates.

To most of us, W. L. Gore and Associates makes those "cool" jackets, pants and other sports clothes items that we wear hunting, fishing, and skiing. You know, the water-repellent, but breathable type of stuff—the kind that lets the sweat out but keeps the cold and rain out. But, Gore-Tex was not the first product of W. L. Gore and Associates ever made.

From the very beginning, in 1958, Wilbert (Bill) Lee Gore and his wife, Genevieve (Vieve) were a team. Bill spent the previous 16 years with DuPont, involved with flouropolymer research. He decided to form his own company, patenting a product called Multi-Tet cable, a product used in computers and process control equipment. From there it grew to its current state of 9,000 employees, with revenues of over 2.5 billion annually.

Though the product mix of the company was exciting and new, it was the culture of teams and teamwork that contributed to the company being regularly named by *Fortune* magazine as one of the top *100 Best Companies to Work For.* In its early years, Gore's culture and success with small teams contributed greatly to the company's success. In 1958, organizing small teams to solve big problems was rare.

Bill organized his company as a flat, lattice-like organization. Everyone shared the same title of "associate." There were no chains of command and "leaders" replaced "bosses." There was a peer-level evaluation system of associates that looked like this:

- Associates are free to encourage, help and allow other associates to grow in knowledge, skill, and scope of responsibility.
- Associates demonstrate fairness to each other and others they come in contact with.
- Associates make their own commitments, but they are expected to keep those they make.
- A waterline situation involves consultation with other associates before taking actions that could impact the reputation or profitability of the company and possibly "sink the ship."

In this team-based organization, people with skills and talents organized themselves around problems and tasks where their interests and talents could be best leveraged. As time passed, leaders evolved as they gained followers and the culture became a kind of pick-your-own leader. Thus, the organization regularly emerged as one of the top organizations for which people wanted to work.

The question to ask yourself is, "As an individual, what do I need to learn and get better at to be a team player?" Here are seven steps you can take to improve your teamwork skills:

1. Look for opportunities to be a contributing part of existing teams within your group or organization.
2. Know your strengths—know what you bring to any team.
3. Know that, while you may be good at what you do, there are others that are better from whom you can learn.
4. Look for opportunities to help any member of your team.
5. Work at developing your contribution; i.e., helping the team to get focused and stay focused, or solving a problem that stands in the way of the team goal or relationship building among team members.
6. You can't be an expert at everything, so choose your teams wisely.
7. Always work to be a positive force.

Finally, it is important to realize that superior performers seldom talk about themselves. The Big "L" is a forgotten word in the vocabulary of star performers.

You will notice those who consistently "out-perform" others—referring to achievements—are those who use the "we" in the organization. In a team photo, the superior performers will be in the last row of team members.

Chapter Seven

PERSPECTIVE—*GETTING THE BIG PICTURE*

Superior performers definitely have a view much different from the mediocre.

In my opinion, too many talented people never reach or become superior performers—because they never get the "big picture." They are 15-year employees with a one-year experience repeated 15 times. They have never moved on from what they first learned. They are mediocre performers.

While the mediocre have limited vision and seldom think beyond the bounds of what they know, superior performers will go beyond and think outside-the-box. They have what I call "outside-the-STAR" thinking. The following is a picture depicting an "outside-the-STAR" thinker.

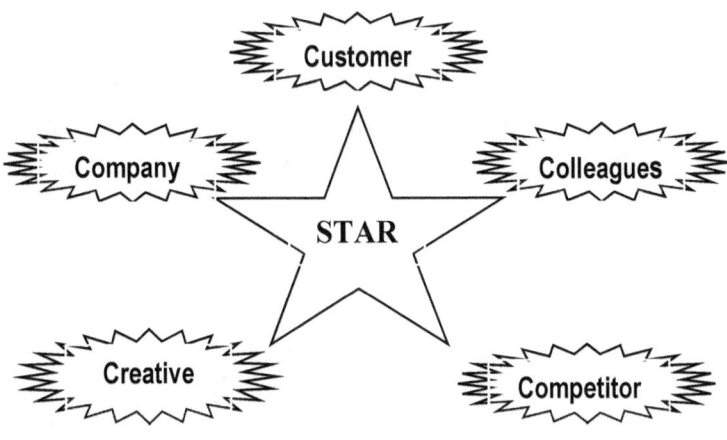

The Five Cs of a superior performer's perspective are all outside-the-Star. The superior performer (the star performer) will give serious consideration to their customers, their company, and their colleagues as well as be creative and competitive. By doing these five steps, STAR performers will distance themselves from the mediocre.

The Colleague Perspective

One of the most important parts of getting the big picture rests with superior performers knowing what they don't know, and realizing that to be the best at what they do, they must build knowledge-resources outside their own group. Resources they can depend upon to give straight and honest feedback when called upon.

The Customer Perspective

Superior performers are capable of seeing things through their customers' eyes. They work to understand their customers' wants and needs and can tie that into the outcome without being overly influential.

The Creative Perspective

Superior performers are unafraid of borrowing from others to meet the needs of their job. They look to other industries, nature and God for inspiration to keep them and their company on "the cutting edge."

The Competitor Perspective
You must be willing to acknowledge that competitors may, on occasion, be better than you are. Be open to seeing and understanding what your competition is doing.

The Company Perspective
Learn how to think like the decision makers. Value their point of view. Know what your boss's goals are and how you can help achieve their goals. Zig Ziglar once said, "If you help enough people reach their goals, you will have no trouble reaching yours."

A final thought about perspective—mediocre performers become superior performers when they master perspective from the viewpoint of The Five "Cs."

Stephen J. Blakesley

CHAPTER EIGHT

SUCCESS—*THE PROGRESSIVE MOVEMENT TOWARD A WORTHY GOAL*

It was Earl Nightingale who I first heard define success. What I have drawn from his definition is that the road is often better than the inn. The journey is more exciting than the destination. Moving closer to your goal daily is success in itself.

The problem most people and organizations face is daily motivation. To remain motivated, you must wake up every morning with a determination to move closer to your goal or objective. If your goal was to maximize the impact of "*The Magnificent Seven*," for instance, how could you best do that? Here are some experience-driven recommendations:

- First, have goals.
- Know why the goals are important to you.
- Visualize how you would be and feel when you achieve your goals.
- Have an action plan to achieve your goals.
- Do something every day or regularly to move yourself closer to your goals.
- Never give up!

Stephen J. Blakesley

Goals and Success Go Together
Without goals or objectives there can be no success. If you have no objectives, you will never know when you have achieved them. Having goals is good, but having written goals is even better. In fact, only three percent of the population of the United States has written goals and Brian Tracy says, "The rest of the world works for them."

Well, maybe not all of the remaining 97 percent works for people with written goals, but there is more to writing goals than meets the eye. Writing goals involves more of the senses than just holding them in your head. It involves seeing goals, feeling goals (through the writing process), and referring to them often. Re-reading them, repeatedly, will help you to remember what is important.

Knowing Why the Goal Is Important
Giving enough thought to a goal to understand why it is important to you is essential to your achieving the goal. If it is not important enough to get your attention, it is not important.

Visualize Achievement of Your Goal
Top athletes use a technique called VMBR (*Visual Motor Behavior Rehearsal)* to help them reach their goals. VMBR involves visualizing the behavior (actions) necessary to achieve your goals. For instance, if you want to be the next CEO of your company, using VMBR, you would research the attributes of great leaders and begin to emulate their behavior mentally, over and over. Then, you would visualize yourself applying those behaviors, and finally, actually doing them. Being able to visualize how you would need to act or behave to achieve your

goal is important because the mind, if you visualize in detail, does not know the difference between visualization and the actual act.

Know Your Action Plan

Before you can visualize you must have a sense of what it takes to achieve your goal. Many people have goals, but that is as far as they go. They do not have the "foggiest" idea about how they would go about achieving them. Goals without action plans are called *wishes*.

Do Something Every Day

One thing you should do every day if you are serious about achieving your goals is to look at them. Actually, you should do more than just look; you should review them and ask yourself, "How am I doing?" Then you should strategize on what you will do today that is likely to move you closer to your goal.

Never Give Up

Three words that almost guarantee goal achievement are "Never give up!" I like to tell people that I have accomplished most of my goals in life, not necessarily on the original time schedule, but I kept on going (like the EverReady bunny) and finally reached them. Just because you don't reach them on time doesn't mean you have lost, it just means that you need to stay focused.

There you have it, a comprehensive plan for application of the seven most important work habits common among superior performers—"The Magnificent Seven."

Stephen J. Blakesley

ABOUT THE AUTHOR

Stephen J. Blakesley

Stephen Blakesley has spent many years in the corporate world developing systems that bring unprecedented successes to all who use them. He is a pioneer in the new science of talent selection and performance. He is acclaimed as an expert at talent-management and performance-management. His events greatly advance the abilities of all attendees. He is recognized as a leader in defining and applying Emotional Intelligence. His corporate training programs are customized to fit your culture.

Contact The Author

14550 Torrey Chase, Ste. 256,
Houston, TX,
77014
Website: **www.gmstalent.com**
Email: **info@gmstalent.com**
281.444.5050

We Thank You!

The Performance People

Stephen J. Blakesley

Performance at the Highest Level

Stephen J. Blakesley

www.ingramcontent.com/pod-product-compliance
Lightning Source LLC
Chambersburg PA
CBHW071717170526
45165CB00005B/2044